JEWISH VOICES IN
UNITARIAN UNIVERSALISM

JEWISH VOICES IN UNITARIAN UNIVERSALISM

Leah Hart-Landsberg and Marti Keller, Editors

SKINNER HOUSE BOOKS

BOSTON

www.skinnerhouse.org

Printed in the United States

Cover and text design by Suzanne Morgan

print ISBN: 978-1-55896-723-6
eBook ISBN: 978-1-55896-724-3

6 5 4 3 2
16 15 14

Library of Congress Cataloging-in-Publication Data

Jewish voices in Unitarian Universalism / Leah Hart-Landsberg and Marti Keller, editors.
    pages cm
"Collection of personal essays by Jewish Unitarian Universalists about their experiences in the faith"—ECIP summary.
ISBN 978-1-55896-723-6 (pbk. : alk. paper)—ISBN 978-1-55896-724- s3 (ebook) 1. Unitarian Universalists—Biography. 2. Jewish Christians—Biography. 3. Unitarian Universalists—Religious life. 4. Jewish Christians—Religious life. 5. Unitarian Universalist churches—Relations—Judaism. 6. Judaism—Relations—Unitarian Universalist churches. 7. Unitarian Universalists for Jewish Awareness. I. Hart-Landsberg, Leah, editor of compilation. II. Keller, Marti, editor of compilation.
  BX9867.J48 2014
  289.1'32089924—dc23
                                    2013033320

For the mixed people who inspire and encourage me:

My sister Rose Hart-Landsberg, spouse Amy Abugo Ongiri, friend Mitra Rahnema, and mentor Ibrahim Abdurrahman Farajajé

—Leah

To Rev. Harold Rosen, who by his presence in the pulpit in Berkeley, California, first showed me the Jewish face of UU ministry.

To the L'Chaim Jewish Celebrations and Awareness Group at the Unitarian Universalist Congregation of Atlanta, who have modeled the power of affinity groups based in our Jewish source and identity for twenty years.

To my husband and children, each one of them Jewish in their own way.

—Marti

CONTENTS

INTRODUCTION

Welcome to this small slice of Unitarian Universalist Jewish community! Whatever path has led you here—whether you are Unitarian Universalist (UU), Jewish, UU Jew, curious passer-by, or firm ally—the editors and contributors of this volume are glad you're here. "Enter, rejoice and come in," as we sing at each worship service at the Fox Valley UU Fellowship in Appleton, Wisconsin, where Leah serves as one of the ministers.

This collection of essays explores the blessings and challenges of Jewish Unitarian Universalist identity and community. Throughout the history of Unitarian Universalism, Jewish heritage, culture, and people have been a consistent presence—one that persists to the present day. This comes as a surprise to many—even those who are UU and Jewish —because there are so few songs, services, books, articles, seminary classes, or other resources that reflect this reality. Giving voice to this community's lived experiences is an act of confident construction; we seek to strengthen UU Judaism, Unitarian Universalism, Judaism, and multi-religious engagement by contributing from our struggles and wisdom.

The first major gathering of the UU Jewish community in over twenty-five years was held in 2011 at the UU Congregation of Atlanta, where Marti served as one of the ministers. The weekly Torah reading that coincided with the *Shabbat* (Sabbath day) of our gathering was *Ki Tisa*, Exodus 30:11–34:35. This text shares instructions for the counting of the Jewish community. And indeed, in gathering as an explicitly UU Jewish group, we were coming together to count ourselves. In doing so, we affirmed our existence.

From counting we turn to the next logical step: sharing not only our numbers but our stories. In this book, we celebrate, wrestle with, and accept the task of our belonging to both Unitarian Universalism and Judaism. There is both unity and diversity in our experiences and perspectives. Let us be counted! Let our voices be heard!

As we know from the Passover traditions, it can be powerful to ask (and answer) four questions. And so each writer shapes their essay as an inquiry into one of the following:

1. As a Jewish Unitarian Universalist, how do you define your identity? How did you come to it? What have been meaningful moments in your journey?
2. How does the Jewish source tradition feed, nurture, inspire, and challenge Unitarian Universalism? How might it do so in the future?

3. How does the Jewish idea of *tikkun olam* (repairing the world) inform your theology, beliefs, and values? Does this concept permeate Unitarian Universalism —how can or should it do so?

4. Have you encountered joy, blessing, and comfort as a UU Jew? What about moments of pain, discomfort, and alienation? How do you grapple with them?

We hope you will ask and answer these questions along with us, keeping the conversations in mind as you move through the world. Much as we sought to include a wide range of voices, any project that involves listening must also try to hear the silence. Those who could claim both Unitarian Universalism and Judaism, yet feel unable or unwilling to make a home in Unitarian Universalism, were hardest to locate. When found, they tended to be reluctant to speak from a UU platform about the heartbreak and hostility they encountered. We acknowledge them here now.

If you asked each writer who they are, they would probably answer with unique words and from different locations. But we all hold in common that we are Mixed People, living within and between Unitarian Universalism and Judaism but decidedly part of both. Our stories are too complex and vibrant to be contained within one simple definition, and yet they are vital. We tell them here.

Leah Hart-Landsberg
Marti Keller

Embracing "And"

Jaclyn Kottman

"You have to pick one." Sarah stared blankly at me from the aisle side of our sticky leather seat. The bus lurched to a stop before continuing on its predetermined track, to let us off, one by one, into our weekends.

"No I don't," my fourth-grade self said insistently, already tired of what felt like round three. "People can celebrate whatever holidays they want."

"But that doesn't make any sense! Either you go to church and you celebrate Christmas, or you go to temple or whatever and you celebrate *Chanukah*. You can't do both. Pick one."

I paused to consider the choices and wished she'd offered *c) None of the above*. "What about celebrating Chanukah *at* church?" I asked.

Again with the blank stare. Then, simply, "No."

I realized something that day that I've often been reminded of throughout my journey toward embracing my

1

religious identity—there's no sense in multiple choice when you need room to write out a short answer or, better yet, an essay.

As with so many Unitarian Universalists, my religious journey began with a question. Not my own, but my parents'. Coming from two very different traditions, they sought a religious home where they could raise a family—one that appreciated their diverse heritage and provided room for their children to follow their own spiritual quests. Their question, "Where is our religious home?" did not have an easy answer. Most churches, temples, synagogues, and congregations in the Deep South did not embrace both Jewish and Christian perspectives as contributing equally to a tapestry of traditions. They finally found the Unitarian Universalist Congregation of Atlanta (UUCA) one Sunday in December, where the service began with the lighting of three symbolic sources of spiritual light: the chalice, an advent wreath, and a *menorah*. They knew they had discovered their common faith. My mother, in particular, remembers being filled that morning with a feeling of acceptance for the universal beauty and significance of Jewish traditions, which she wove into our family life.

For my brothers and me, religious pluralism was as much a part of our lives as the Southern drawl that flavored our interactions. We spent Friday evenings at the dinner table, often with a loaf of raisin *challah* from the grocery bakery, or with pizza and the latest episode of Star Trek, and we put our own spin on the Sabbath prayers and songs that marked the end of the week. We celebrated our cousins' *bar* and *bat mitzvahs* and our friends' first communions. We ended Passover at Nana's house with songs, stories, and prayers that served as a prelude to the classic combination of brisket, green beans, squash casserole, and sweet tea. We marked Easter with morning services, followed by a backyard egg hunt and a colorful midday dinner of fluorescent Jell-O eggs, purple mashed potatoes, and our annual "bunny cake." December meant a flurry of revolving decorations between birthdays, Chanukah, and Christmas in a variety of chronological combinations, given that particular year's calendar. And each year at High Holy Days we observed *Rosh Hashanah* and *Yom Kippur* at UUCA with services led by L'Chaim, the Jewish Celebrations Group. It was at those services and in the unmistakably sweet taste of apples and honey that I discovered a deep connection with my Jewish heritage that I could not explain or ignore. I was so proud to say, "Please read responsively" into the microphone at the pulpit, to hear my brother create the piercing sound of the shofar as it rang through our circular sanctuary, and to listen to my mother lead the singing in her clear, passionate voice. I felt an intangible connection to something bigger than myself that I didn't feel at any other time of the year. The haunting half-step that marked the beginning of the *Kol Nidre* immediately connected me not only to my family and to everyone gathered in that space made holy by our worship, but to thousands of years of human history. I felt a sense of wholeness, of connectedness with my spirituality that was unlike anything else. I felt at home within myself.

While the question, "What *are* you?" came from the well-intentioned curiosity of my friends at school, it felt like a challenge to the legitimacy of my plural religious identity. Jewish friends chided, "Why do you even care about Yom Kippur? You're not a *real* Jew," not understanding that I wasn't trying to be Jewish. Other friends seemed really puzzled by the menorah that shone next to our Christmas tree in the living room window, or the glittery Stars of David and carved wooden chalices that hung as ornaments on the Christmas tree branches. Yet while many people told me that this combination of Judaism and Unitarian Universalism didn't make any sense, so many others encouraged me to embrace the "and" rather than the "or." My Sunday School teachers, ministers, mentors, and parents guided me as I spirituality developed within a community that encouraged me to explore rather than limit myself. "What is it about both Judaism and Unitarian Universalism that speaks to you?" they asked, an encouragement to go on a deep search for what was true and right for me.

Eventually, I stopped listening to those who seemed to be stuck on the What's and Why's. I learned that, by embracing the Who at the center of it all, I could discover beautiful and meaningful traditions that feed my spirit. I included Hebrew in my Coming of Age credo statement, a UU tradition where youth share deeply in worship about their personally constructed systems of belief. I figured out how to use yeast and started baking homemade raisin challah. I went on my own *tashlich*, walking each fall along the river in my Midwest college town with crackers in my pocket and casting them into the water, each year with a list of different intentions. I ate peanut butter, *matzah*, and jelly sandwiches for a week in the spring and raced my friends in reading "*Chad Gadya*" as fast as we possibly could on one breath during the Passover *Seders* held on our college campus. Away from where I grew up, in the town that has become my new home, I attend High Holy Day services each year at the local synagogue. "Oh, are you Jewish?" some of my fellow worshippers have asked. "Yes and no," I answer with pride. "I'm a Jewish Unitarian Universalist."

—o—

JACLYN KOTTMAN *is a music educator in Appleton, Wisconsin, where she attends the Fox Valley Unitarian Univeralist Fellowship. She hopes to take a page out of her mother's book and add to the spiritual mosaic of her new Unitarian Universalist home by helping to start a Jewish Celebrations group—where all are welcome to draw their own meaning from the beautiful traditions of Judaism. This essay is for Marcia Fishman, a proud Jewish Unitarian Universalist and spiritual teacher, who showed all who were blessed to know her how to live with passion, grace, and strength.*

ILLUSTRIOUS ANCESTORS

ROB ELLER-ISAACS

Our sense of ancestry or tribe is key to our identity. And there is a complex constellation of issues surrounding Jewish identity in particular. The history of pogroms and prejudice culminating in the Holocaust, the deep ambivalence progressive people feel about the State of Israel, and the all-too-human tendency to box each other in with narrow definitions all combine to make writing about Jewish identity perilous.

I was born in 1951 on the South Side of Chicago to a Reform Jewish family. My mother's family was Czech/Russian. They had come to the United States following the Franco-Prussian war (1870–71). The family was culturally Jewish but did not practice. My father's family was German, Dutch, and English. They came over in the 1840s, settling in New York and Toronto. By the late 1890s, my father's parents had settled in Chicago. My grandfather was staunchly secular. His mother called herself a "Hirschite" because of her devotion to Rabbi Emil Hirsch of Temple Sinai. A pioneer of Reform Judaism in the United States, he was known for his progressive commitments, for his interfaith work, and for famously saying at the end of a *Yom Kippur* service, "Fast if you wish. I'm going home to dine with my family."

When I was very young, my family, including my paternal grandmother, were members of Kehilath Anshe Ma'arav (Congregation of the Men of the West), also known as KAM. The Temple and its rabbi, Jacob Weinstein, were among the founding partners of the Hyde Park/Kenwood Community Conference. They also supported Saul Alinsky in the early days of the Woodlawn Organization, a group formed in the Industrial Areas Foundation tradition of building social change power. In our neighborhood, the Jews and the Unitarians were among those most deeply involved in the early days of the civil rights movement. When my sister was eleven (and I was five), a friend from school invited her to come for a Sunday to the First Unitarian Society of Chicago. That day, the Sunday School class was acting out a section of the Book of Exodus. Knowing that Janie was Jewish, they asked if she would like to be Moses. A budding feminist even at eleven, she was delighted to comply. She never looked back.

In 1956, Christopher Moore, a minister at the Unitarian Church in Hyde Park, established a children's choir there. My sister Jane joined that year. Chris had a vision. He wanted to build a world-class choir, intentionally integrated across lines of race and class. He wanted to provide both a literal and symbolic image of harmony, which would inspire solidarity and social harmony among all those with ears to hear and eyes to see. He did just that. When I was seven, old enough to audition, I joined the choir too.

My grandmother became concerned. We were spending an awful lot of time at a place that called itself a church. We were clearly drifting away from Judaism. She went to see Rabbi Weinstein to ask his advice. As family lore has it, Weinstein replied, "Sophie, nothing worse should ever happen to you than that your grandchildren sing with the Unitarians."

So sing we did, and as we sang, we gave concrete expression to the beloved community. In 1960 the choir became a partner in an organization called Urban Gateways. Every third grader in Chicago was invited to audition. We became the Chicago Children's Choir. Chris's dream became a reality. The choir was the center of our lives. And the choir's church became the closest thing we had to a religious community. We left Judaism behind without as much as a nod of farewell.

And yet, I have always considered myself to be Jewish. I have vivid memories of standing in my place singing the old words to "For All the Saints" and choking on *Jesus*. "Thy name O . . ." Despite my parent's liberalism, despite the ease with which we folded our lives into the Unitarian Church, I still felt like a traitor. Somewhere inside me a disembodied voice kept saying, "You have betrayed us."

When my voice changed and I could no longer sing with the choir, the bottom dropped out of my world. The church caught me as I fell. There was a strong, active, integrated youth group at the church. The sense of beloved community I had experienced in the choir continued in LRY (Liberal Religious Youth). We were passionately involved in civil rights and later in the struggle to end the war in Viet Nam. Questions of religious identity were overshadowed by, as Dr. Martin Luther King Jr. put it at the March on Washington, "the fierce urgency of now." I began to claim Unitarian Universalism as my own. While my name, my sense of humor, and the way I talked with my hands indicated that I was Jewish, when asked, I would say, "I am of Jewish heritage, but now I'm a committed Unitarian Universalist."

Eventually I enrolled at Starr King School for the Ministry. In my third year there, questions about my Jewish identity troubled me again. I began to develop a consistent devotion to spiritual practice and became acutely aware that Unitarian Universalism had little spiritual discipline to offer. My disappointment was greater than the usual disgruntlement seminarians suffer when they compare the actual church to the idealized form they're taught in school to treasure. Spiritual practice was becoming my lifeline. I was struggling with existential emptiness. I was drifting. I was lonely. I was anxious, and my church had nothing to offer beyond hard work or psychotherapy. I needed more.

Some of my friends turned to what theologian Harvey Cox called "the new orientalism." They took up chanting,

yoga, or sitting meditation. A few became "Jesus freaks."
I decided to explore Judaism—not the Reform Judaism
of my family, but *Hasidism*: the mystical, orthodox, dis-
ciplined, impassioned Jewish tradition established by the
Baal Shem Tov in the eighteenth century. I was drawn to it
through *Tales of the Early Masters*, an anthology of whim-
sical koan-like Hasidic stories as told by Martin Buber.
If Unitarian Universalism had no practice path to offer,
perhaps I would find what I was looking for by turning
back toward Judaism.

I was twenty-three years old, living in Boston and serving as a ministerial intern at Arlington Street Church. I
called to arrange a visit to the New England Hasidic Center.
They invited me to join them for *Shabbat* and to stay for
the weekend. Trying to breathe past the butterflies in my
stomach, I took the T out to Brookline, walked the few
blocks to the Synagogue (in Hasidic Judaism there is only
one Temple) and rang the bell. A young *Hasid* answered
the bell. He welcomed me warmly and led me to the imposing double doors that led to the rabbi's apartment. His
knock was answered by the rabbi's wife. She looked me up
and down, took in my shoulder length hair and the gold
hoop in my left earlobe, shook her head, and said simply,
"Follow me."

It was a spacious apartment, with that particular faded
elegance one finds in places like Budapest and Prague. We
walked through the living room, our footsteps muffled by
worn Persian rugs, the scent of wood-wax in the air. She

knocked and left me standing at his study door. "Come in," he said. I did. "Come sit." I sat. Behind a massive, cluttered, mahogany desk sat Abraham Horowitz, chief rabbi of the New England Hasidic Center. He was an imposing figure, his great white beard set off against an elegant, old black suit. His eyes met mine. Trite as it may sound, I sensed that he saw into my soul. "Have you come to study or just to judge?" he asked. "I don't know yet," I carefully replied. "You are welcome either way. Settle in, I'll see you at dinner."

It turned out that the young Hasid who had met me at the door was assigned to accompany me throughout the weekend. He was my interpreter and guard. His primary duty was to help me stay within the constraints imposed by scripture and tradition. He showed me to my room. I reached up to turn on the light. He said only, "Stop," and grabbed my wrist. As though talking to a child, he then explained that kindling a fire on the Shabbat was forbidden and that electric lights were modern fires. It was the first of many such moments that tilted my time there more toward judgment than study.

From the moment I arrived I was under observation. I had been born a Jew, but what kind of a Jew? Was I Jewish enough? Did I seem open to the teachings? Would I ever make a good Hasid? As the sun set, we gathered at the Shabbat table. This was the moment I had been waiting for. I had warm childhood memories of gathering for *Pesach* with our extended family. What could be more purely Jewish than joining Rabbi Horowitz and his family for Shabbat? We washed in the ritual manner and sat down to dinner. The rabbi's wife said the blessing. *Challah* was broken. Soup was served. Then the rabbi asked, "What is your name?" "Robert Lewis Isaacs," I replied. "And your father's name?" he asked. "Alexander Josephi Isaacs." "You see," he said, addressing the others at the table, "his family has drifted so far from faith that both he and his father have foreign names. If he stays, we will have to give them both new names. We'll make them real Jews again."

In that moment, I remembered a dear friend, also a Unitarian Universalist of Jewish ancestry, who, when asked why he had become a Unitarian Universalist, said simply, "Unitarian Universalists are the only people I know who will let me be the Jew I am." I was drawn to the stories. I was drawn to the drinking and dancing, the ecstatic worship for which the Hasidic community is known. But I was not looking for a new way of life. I was, and I remain, deeply grounded in Unitarian Universalist identity. I don't need or want anyone to judge my level of compliance with some caricature of Jewish identity.

One of the great strengths of our tradition is that we affirm each person's right and responsibility to construct their own identity. In his 2006 book *Identity and Violence: The Illusion of Destiny*, Nobel Prize-winning economist Amartya Sen makes a compelling case for cultivating a worldview that celebrates "diverse identities." He asks us to refuse to be involved in what he calls "the miniaturization of human beings." He argues that we diminish other people when we make assumptions about them based on the notion that their behavior results from a determinant, singular identity.

"Since what we choose is what we are….," the old hymn claims. I don't know whether Unitarian Universalism has chosen me or I have chosen it. But here I am. I treasure our openness to what Sen calls "diverse identities." I treasure our small part in encouraging the expansion of human agency, freedom, and choice. I am humbled by the fact that we too tend to define ourselves too narrowly. We too live in the tension between our tendency for like-minded tribalism and our longing for beloved community.

I stayed the night at the New England Hasidic Center to be polite. I hadn't planned to go to church that Sunday. But I couldn't stay away. I just wanted to be there to say thank you, thank you to my family for having the strength to break free, thank you to Unitarian Universalism for helping me move toward authenticity, thank you to Jake Weinstein for telling my dear grandmother that we all were going to be okay.

—◦—

ROB ELLER-ISAACS *began his career at the Unitarian Society of Whittier, California. In 1982 he and his wife and colleague, Janne, moved to Oakland, where they stayed for eighteen years. Their ministry there helped to expand Unitarian Universalism's understanding and practice of shared ministry. In 2000, they* *moved to Saint Paul, Minnesota, where they are co-ministers of Unity Church, Unitarian, serving in innovative and transforming ways.*

TAMBOURINES AND TESHUVAH

DARA OLANDT

Miriam, dance with us in order to repair the world.
            —Rabbi Leila Gal Berner

Unitarian Universalists come from many religious and cultural backgrounds. We use diverse language to refer to the sense of the sacred in our lives. Raised both Unitarian Universalist and Jewish, on my own path I have found it powerful to reconnect with Jewish roots and explore stories from my faith forebears.

Unearthing and reclaiming archetypal stories from Jewish texts have inspired me to carefully unpack my own relationships to Jewish identity and practice. Today, I claim a more whole and authentic Unitarian Universalist self-identity, one that includes an embrace of my Jewishness. This grounds me as human being, a person and as a Unitarian Universalist minister in the twenty-first century.

In Hebrew there is a word *teshuvah,* which means return.

It can also be translated as "repentance" or "atonement" (alternatively spelled "at-one-ment"). The journey to rediscover my own connection with Jewishness is a process of ever-deepening teshuvah. Growing up bi-religiously, I did not learn much about these words. As a child, I also didn't have much familiarity with stories from the Hebrew Bible or a particular affinity for characters like famous Moses or his unsung sister, Miriam.

In the Hebrew Bible, there are only a handful of stories about Miriam, the mysterious sister of Moses. Over the years, Jewish women have developed stories about Miriam, filling in the gaps in with what could be gleaned about her from the scarce references found in ancient texts. According to the stories, Miriam escaped from slavery in Egypt. After the long, arduous, and improbable crossing of the Red Sea, resilient Miriam picked up her tambourine. She played loudly and with joy upon the shores of freedom. Doing so, she encouraged her kin to dance and sing.

Miriam nourished the exhausted with inspiration; her encouragement offered them hope. She was a spiritual leader in her own right. Certain interpretations of ancient stories tell of "Miriam's well." This well is said to have followed the wanderers as they sojourned across the parched desert. The water from her well quenched the spiritual thirst of exiles in the wilderness.

Today, some people add a goblet of water to the traditional *Seder* plate at Passover. "Miriam's cup" symbolizes spiritual rejuvenation, especially in times of hardship. An archetype of spiritual renewal, Miriam recalls the importance of music and praise, the presence of possibility, and the persistence of beauty even in times of loss, despair, and suffering.

Miriam interests me, as does the ways she has been lifted up and creatively (re)imagined. Perhaps this is because I was raised Unitarian Universalist and Jewish in a family ambivalent about our own Jewish identity yet intrinsically shaped by it. Growing up, I struggled to shape or imagine a meaningful identity from the complex and mixed messages regarding Jewishness that I encountered in my young life.

As a child, on alternate weekends I attended our local Unitarian Universalist church and the Yale Hillel Children's School for Reformed and interfaith Jewish families. I gallivanted through the halls of the Unitarian Universalist congregation with my siblings. The building seemed an extension of our living room, the people our family. From earliest memory, Unitarian Universalism meant sensory experiences: eating donuts at coffee hour, exploring "world religions" through art projects, singing in worship, and playing games at the all-congregation retreat in the summer. So my young Unitarian Universalist identity was formed, then, not by explicit theology, but by experiencing life within a warm, multigenerational community.

Weekends when I was not at UU Sunday School, I attended Hebrew classes taught by valiant young student rabbis. Despite their hard work, I stumbled over the language. Awed and intimidated by the somber voice of the cantor, I felt a persistent distance from religious Judaism.

Jewish identity, on the whole, seemed an elusive puzzle. So I listened for clues about Jewish identity in family stories. My *Ashkenazi* Jewish family, of Eastern European descent, told many stories that revealed the tensions of assimilation in the United States: individuals changing names to avoid being "outed" as Jewish, others converting to Christianity or not practicing Judaism. In the 1940s members of the KKK burned a cross in front of my cousin's home. This side of my family included some of the first Jews to open a dry goods store in the South.

As a child, my Jewish identity occurred to me as a problematic sort of fate. In middle school, I digested a glut of popular young adults books focused on stories about children fleeing Nazis during the Holocaust. It is hard to communicate just how powerful these stories and images were in my child imagination. As a result, I developed an unfortunate understanding that "Jewishness" was scary, perhaps even dangerous.

At thirteen, I finished my *bat mitzvah*. Following this rite of passage, I did not readily enter a synagogue, except for an occasional High Holidays service, for over ten years.

I was well on my way to becoming a UU minister when I became inspired to embark upon an intentional journey of teshuva, or return; to unpack my own and what I could discern of my family's complicated relationship to Jewish identity and practice. It was Unitarian Universalism that inspired me to re-examine my Jewish roots and helped me to dissolve the negative messages I had earlier internalized about my own Jewish identity. Over several years, this teshuva journey opened for me a deeper connection with my own Jewish heritage, and led to a more vibrant, robust appreciation for Unitarian Universalism.

Antiracism and counter-oppressive work called me to research how my family in the United States moved from identifying as Jewish and "other" in some generations to "passing" in later generations, with varying degrees of success, into Caucasian middle-class culture.

Many good resources aided this research. Karen Brodkin's groundbreaking book *How Jews Became White Folks: And What That Says About Race in America* explores the various ways Jewish people have self-defined and have experienced "Jewishness" in this country over time. Incorporating critical race theory, sociological research, and oral histories from her family and others, Brodkin argues that construction and interpretation of Jewish ethnoracial identities are affected by a shifting context of ethnoracial assignment—what the dominant power assigns, based upon economic, political, cultural, geographic, and other factors, and nuanced by class, age, and gender.

Brodkin's work illustrates the fluid understandings of Jewish identity. She suggests that individual Jewish ethnoracial identity in the United States may be experienced differently by people in the same family—or even in multiple ways by one person in different contexts. For example, someone from an Ashkenazi background who experiences Jewishness as an ethnoracial assignment may continue to identify as enthnoracially Jewish; yet only two generations later, a grandchild of the same person may unblinkingly self-identify as "white" or "Caucasian" (the ethnoracial Jewish identification now erased, or possibly an afterthought).

Brodkin's larger historical analysis shows the ways that the distribution of GI benefits in World War II aided many Ashkenazi Jews in ascending into the ranks of the middle-class, assimilating as white and thereby gaining economic privileges previously unavailable to them (and denied to those who continued to be assigned as "others" in the United States). My own family followed this pattern of enthnoracialized economic mobility, but our family stories reveal a chronic uneasiness with this transition.

Brodkin writes,

> Prevailing classifications at a particular time have sometimes assigned us to the white race, and at other times have created an off-white race for Jews to in-habit. Changes in our racial assignment have shaped the ways in which American Jews who have grown up in different eras understand our ethnoracial iden-tities. Those changes give us a kind of double vision that comes from racial middleness: of an experience of marginality vis-à-vis whiteness and experience of whiteness vis-à-vis blackness.

Here, her description of "racial middleness" and "double vision" found within constructions of Jewish identity helped me make sense of my own family's narratives, and the pervasive sense of liminality, or "inbetweeness," that makes our Jewish identity complex.

This critical work by Brodkin and others helped me parse through my own personal narratives of Jewishness with new clarity. Yet, it was music that awakened me, liberating for me the most fulfilling reconnection to my Jewish heritage.

One auspicious Friday evening, while in seminary, I accepted an invitation to attend services at a local Jewish Renewal community in Berkeley, California. As I opened the door, I was greeted with laughing, dancing, and boisterous singing. Children and elders clapped hands. People in the room had straight hair, wavy hair, and many had curly hair (just like my own!). Those gathered visibly reflected the racial and ethnic diversity of the neighborhood itself. The room filled with words in a language distantly familiar to my ears. *Hebrew.*

I was unprepared for this multicultural, twenty-first-century Jewish Renewal service, with its embrace of Ashkenazi and Sephardic music and embodied devotional practices. The words to prayers were translated to be gender inclusive. It was here that I encountered for the very first time the English translation of the Hebrew letters for "God," spelled "G-D," to express the idea that God cannot be described fully by any human language.

As I sat down in the back row, a wave of appreciation hit my heart and tears sprung to my eyes. It was not like any synagogue I had ever been to. I had been estranged, for over twenty years, from an authentic connection to the

Jewish portion of my UU-Jewish identity. Later, I brought my mother and sister and each of them remarked on how healing it was to experience this kind of joyful, spiritually enlivening Jewish service.

Jewish identities are diverse, multifold, and fluid. The spiritually alive and particularly engaging Jewish *Shabbat* service reminded me that no experience of religion must be static or frozen. Today, my UU-Jewish identity calls me to more fully embrace my own wholeness and with this comes a responsibility to continuously practice dissolving inner barriers while joyously calling upon others to do the same.

We Unitarian Universalists are changing, dynamic people, in a changing, growing world. In the twenty-first century, we are a plural people with many cultural, lingual, racial, and ethnic identities. At its best, I understand that our shared tradition, Unitarian Universalism, points us toward that which is most life-affirming, life-giving, and liberating. With its emphasis on self-inquiry and an ambitious embrace of pluralism, Unitarian Universalism has inspired me to explore a more complex identity as a human being and to repair my own arrested development of an authentic Jewish sense of self.

A vibrant Unitarian Universalist religious movement of today and tomorrow means, I believe, a "big tabernacle" home where we can bring the fullness of our lives, with our complex, multifaceted identities, our plural ways of knowing, being, singing, praising, praying, meditating, inquiring, wrestling, and growing. In diverse cultural, lingual, and theological ways, we can bring our full, human selves with us to Unitarian Universalism. It may not always be easy, but it is vital.

If I were to add my own flourish to the legends told about Miriam, I would suggest that when Miriam lifts her tambourine to play, she plays not for herself nor her people's liberation alone. Instead, she plays for all who are on an unsure path, who, weary and exhausted, find themselves in the borderlands, washed up on the shores of a tenuous and treasured freedom. Her tambourine plays with a profound sweetness. A sweetness born of both hard memories and hope, filled with thanksgiving for a sense of precious deliverance.

When I think of Miriam and her tambourine, I am reminded of those who have come before, as well as those who journey together in the present, and those yet to come, with the blessings and challenges of the terrain ahead, with its new, bright, deep music.

―◂◦▸―

DARA OLANDT *serves as the minister of the Unitarian Universalist Congregation in Blacksburg, Virginia. She is a lifelong Unitarian Universalist of Jewish heritage and practice. She was raised in the Main Line Unitarian Universalist Church of Devon, Pennsylvania, and concurrently attended the Yale Hillel Children's Program, where she became a bat mitzvah. She is a graduate of Starr King School for the Ministry.*

LIVING IN AMBIGUITY

DENISE TAFT DAVIDOFF

Years and years ago, my brother sailed from Connecticut to Nantucket with my husband Jerry and me. He was a dashing bachelor at the time and, when we arrived at The Jetties beach to spend the afternoon, Jerry and I gravitated to the family side, to visit with friends and their young children, while my brother Jim went off to look over the field on the singles side. Later that night, back on the boat, Jim said only half in jest that it was a burden to be James Gordon Taft: "I always want to say to a girl I'm talking to, 'Don't worry, dear, I'm actually Jewish.' You were so smart to take Jerry's name when you got married."

It's true. I was very intentional about trading in my Denise Ellen Taft identity for Denise Davidoff back in 1955. Like my brother, I wanted a fast way to let people know I was Jewish. I've never regretted that decision. But it did get a bit more complicated when I chose to be further identified as Unitarian Universalist, starting in the early sixties.

I left the synagogue life of my childhood because of a theological and liturgical quarrel. I could no longer say or believe the *Shema. Hear O Israel: the Lord thy God, the Lord Is One*. I questioned the concept of God. I questioned the language of *Lord*. I questioned the whole deal. In my college years, I had become an agnostic and a humanist. I was ripe for what I later found in The Unitarian Church in Westport, Connecticut. But I never stopped being a cultural Jew and a Zionist. I never stopped celebrating the holidays that joined me to the people and the traditions of both my father's and mother's families, to whom I was and am still devoted. I abandoned rigid theological tenets and patriarchal worship practices, but I did not abandon my Jewish identity. That was always a keeper for me.

Meaningful moments in my journey have included being the first Jewish moderator of the Unitarian Universalist Association (UUA), reclaiming my theism, living into my Jewishness as one delightful consequence of our institutional striving to make Unitarian Universalism more multicultural.

Michael Chabon, author of many well-received books, including *The Yiddish Policemen's Union*, wrote this in an elegy that appeared in the *New York Times* titled "Chosen But Not Special":

> As a Jewish child, I was regularly instructed, both sub-
> tly and openly, that Jews, the people of Maimonides,
> Albert Einstein, Jonas Salk, and Meyer Lansky, were on
> the whole smarter, cleverer, more brilliant, more astute

than other people. And, duly, I would look around the Passover table, say at the members of my family, and remark on the presence of a number of highly intelligent, quick-witted, shrewd, well-educated people filled to bursting with information, explanations, and opinions on a diverse range of topics. In my tractable and vainglorious eagerness to confirm the People of Einstein theory, my gaze would skip right over—God love them—any counter examples present at that year's Seder. This is why, to a Jew, it always comes as a shock to encounter stupid Jews. . . . The shock comes not because we have never encountered any stupid Jews before—Jews are stupid in roughly the same proportion as all the world's people—but simply because from an early age we have been trained, implicitly and explicitly, to ignore them.

Chabon's reflections recall the Jewishness of my childhood as well. I, too, was carefully taught that we Jews are brilliant. We are successful. We are chosen by God. And that, the *chosenness*, is why we are also persecuted, despised, and envied.

The other powerful Jewish part of my childhood was, *is*, the Exodus story. For as long as I can remember, my father's family gathered on the first night of *Pesach* to recount the hallowed tale. Once we were slaves unto Pharaoh in Egypt and God came to rescue us through Moses, who led us through the desert for forty years, delivered to us the Ten Commandments, and, just before his death, brought us to

Canaan, our homeland. Next year, we will meet in Jerusalem. Slaves everywhere should be set free. Bring on the
festive dinner. Seriously, this was the story at the core of the
justice ethic instilled in my brother and me and all our Taft
cousins. This was the story that fueled my parents' anguish
over the way "negroes" (in the language of my childhood)
were treated in the South. The Ku Klux Klan was like that
Pharaoh. This was the mythology that framed my family's
agony about the Holocaust in Europe. Hitler was like that
Pharaoh, only worse. This was the impetus behind my family's ardent Zionism. We have wandered for too long. We
are aliens in a strange land. We must have a Jewish home.

When I turned sixteen, I began to question the Jewish theology and mythologies of my upbringing. An all
powerful God, really? People of the book, really? The
"chosen," really? And why did the litany and rituals in
our synagogue make me so uncomfortable, so angry and
resentful? Later, much later, when I discovered patriarchy
in thought, language, and practice as an emerging feminist
within Unitarian Universalism, I came to realize that the
theological teachings of my girlhood had been delivered
as part and parcel of a stultifying sexism that ultimately
drove me away. On the horizon was a religious community
that encouraged questioning, seeking the freedom from
orthodoxy I had been thirsting for. Unitarian Universalism.
As a family with two very young children, my husband
and I began to attend The Unitarian Church in Westport
in September 1960 and were soon caught up in a variety

of tasks—teaching religious education, governance, fund raising, growth, liberal community—lots of good stuff.

In 1992, a month past my sixtieth birthday, I put together a Sunday-morning worship service for my colleagues on the UUA Board of Trustees. Yes, the sermon was all about me. What I had come to realize and wanted to share was that my long time dispute with my forefathers—Abraham, Isaac, and Jacob—also involved a lifelong dispute with my birth father, Allen. The patriarchy of my religious community reflected the patriarchy of my childhood home and the combination was toxic. In that sermon, I promised myself with my colleagues as witnesses, that I would give up being angry with my father who, after all, had been dead for twenty-one years. "The anger takes up too much room," I confessed. That turned out to be a promise I could keep, and a good thing it was.

Once I got past rejecting my childhood Judaism, I could relax into more pleasant memories. These included Temple Beth El in the Rockaway Park neighborhood of Queens, New York (a community sadly demolished by Hurricane Sandy), the *Purim* carnival masquerades and prune-stuffed *hamentaschen,* the *Chanukah* celebrations with *dreidels* and singing and delicious *latkes*, the wise teaching offered me as a fifteen-year-old studying for her *Shavuot* confirmation, the warmth of community lavished on the children of that congregation. And I could begin to rethink theism!

Was it a coincidence that the shift in attitude presaged my election as UUA moderator in 1993? No one consulted

with me regarding the details of my installation as moderator on the final day of the 1993 General Assembly in
Charlotte, North Carolina. I had chosen two minister
friends, a married couple, to do the charge. That, and
showing up, appeared to be my tasks. So I was surprised
that the music chosen to announce the beginning of
the ceremony was #220 in *Singing the Living Tradition*,
described as "a Hebrew folk song" and, indeed, a *hora*.
At the time, I was not glad, not mad, just surprised. I
was, after all, the first denominational official who self-
identified as Jewish. The first non-gentile moderator
(still!). So did the installation planners choose "Bring
Out the Festal Bread" to honor my Jewishness, herald
my Jewishness? Label my Jewishness? And why wasn't
the motive spoken of, by them or by me?

I presided at GA for the first time in Fort Worth, Texas,
in June of 1994. The affiliated group Unitarian Universalists
for Jewish Awareness (UUJA) asked me to speak at their
Shabbat service about being a Jewish Unitarian Universalist. I don't particularly remember what I said, but I vividly
recall the testimony during the Q & A that followed from
several UU ministers of Jewish descent about their regular
visits to Shabbat services at home, about incipient anti-
Semitism in the Unitarian Universalist Ministers Association and some of our congregations—corroborated by two
male ministers who were lifelong Unitarians. I averred that
I had not felt anti-Semitism in my years in our movement.
They all thought I was naïve. Now I think they were right.

Beacon Press honored me with a request to write the preface to John Buehrens and Forrest Church's *A Chosen Faith*, which the press was reissuing in 1998. I felt really good about their reason: John and Forrest wanted to appeal to Jews who were considering joining Unitarian Universalist congregations and who might relate to my personal story. I wrote,

Signing the membership book in a Unitarian church was scary beyond belief for me to even contemplate. How would I tell my parents I was rejecting the faith of my forefathers? . . . How would I tell my aunts and uncles and cousins? How would I tell my in-laws? How would I tell our friends, particularly those in the Temple Israel community in our town?

. . . And *what* would I tell them? . . . How to explain how good that simple English language liturgy and those guilt-free uplifting sermons felt in the ears, and, increasingly in the heart? Emerson and Channing and Parker were names mentioned in courses I'd taken in American cultural history at Vassar. But join a *church*? (In my family, if you went to a church, you were a Christian . . .).

The most searing struggle I have had with Jewish identity through the decades since I went to my first service at The Unitarian Church of Fairfield County (as it was then called) in 1960 is that word we call our collective selves, *church*. I have always cringed about labeling myself a *church*-goer. I find ways to avoid using the word, which isn't easy since the name of my congregation is The Unitarian *Church* in Westport. Rarely does a month go by that someone at a dinner party or at the gym or at an organizational meeting speaks to me about their fascination with our faith and their total inability to join a *church.* I have come to understand that this is something I have to live with and make the best of—and I fully "get" why I must. I am a Jewish-identified Unitarian Universalist institutionalist who embraces our need to become multiracial and multicultural. Fighting about gathering in *churches* is not useful to this important initiative. I live in ambiguity. It's not about me.

◄○►

DENISE "DENNY" TAFT DAVIDOFF *was born into a Conservative Jewish family, and her Temple in Belle Harbor, New York, was an important part of her family life and childhood. She attended the religious education program from kindergarten through her confirmation on Shavuot of l947. She attends the Unitarian Church in Westport, Connecticut. Denny was the first Jewish person in UUA governance when she was elected moderator in l993.*

The Almost Unitarian Rabbi

Leah Hart-Landsberg

"**B**ut Mom, which am I—Jewish or Christian or Unitarian Universalist?"

As a child, my sister would come home after being taunted by an aggressively Christian child in the neighborhood and beg our mother to designate a religion—any religion—that would precisely place her in the faith world. My mother would respond that our family was both Jewish and Unitarian Universalist. That it was okay to be both.

So we grew up Unitarian Universalist and Jewish in a family that is both. Yet for many years, I felt I had to pick, as if I couldn't be a Jew and a UU at the same time. What is it about our world that makes us believe we must choose one religious background and faith tradition, as well as one of other identities?

My sister and I aren't unusual in inhabiting a borderland place—but that doesn't mean it's comfortable. How can it be? Our culture is rife with tension surrounding both/and spaces and the people who occupy them. People often feel nervous about those who defy tidy categories of religion, race, gender, ability, and more. Ambiguous territory is scary because it can't be easily understood, regulated, or tucked away. In middle school, when a classmate drew a swastika on my notebook, I felt exposed to the world as a Jew. Since my primary community at the time was Unitarian Universalist, I wasn't sure if those surrounding me would understand or recognize how deeply this anti-Semitism permeated my head and heart. The episode left me feeling hyper-visible and confused.

Unitarian Universalists have long heralded values of diversity, but who among us is immune from discomfort about multiple identities, including plural faith traditions? In seminary, a classmate shared that my failure to sever ties to my Jewish identity and be at home in an exclusively UU community felt like an act of aggression to her because she was a "pure" devotee to our tradition. Later, a congregation I served as minister hosted both a *Pesach Seder* and Easter services. "But we should take down the Passover flyers," said a member as the second holiday neared. "We don't want to confuse or offend those who come for Easter." As someone who lives by combining and straddling religious categories, I suddenly felt a little too complicated and controversial.

In fact, our legacy is all about shades of multi-religious meaning. Both/and-ers have helped shape us into who we are. One story we should tell more often is that of Rabbi

Solomon Hirsch Sonneschein, a long overlooked Jewish UU ancestor. Also known as the Sunshine Rabbi (his last name means sunshine in German), Sonneschein was born in Hungary. In the 1860s, after serving synagogues in Europe, he came to the United States in the early days of the Reform Judaism movement, which began in nineteenth-century Germany and rapidly spread to the United States.

After quickly coming into contact with Unitarians and their ideas, Sonneschein was intrigued. Certainly, the cultural backgrounds of the Unitarians differed sharply from those of the American Jewish Reformers of his own community, who were mostly Central European immigrants and their American-born children. Reformers tended to be socially marginalized, with little access to wealth. What a difference from these Unitarians, who tended to be US natives with extensive economic and ethnic privilege, their culture grounded in Protestant Christianity.

Despite their different backgrounds, Reformers and Unitarians wrestled with the same dilemmas. What's the relationship between our older understandings and the new, radical ideas? How can we redefine our practices to make our worship relevant to the present and future? The two movements also had similar eschatological ideas about what happens at the end of life and time. Is our planet evolving toward some kind of ultimate event or conclusion? Unitarians and Jewish Reformers said no. God has not foreordained a fiery apocalypse. Heaven and hell matter less than living an ethical life, which is worth struggling for here, now.

Recognizing these commonalities, some Unitarian ministers and Reform rabbis started pulpit and *bimah* exchanges. Congregations set up subscription exchanges so they could read each other's publications. Conversations and relationships flourished. Some Jews and Unitarians even began calling for the marriage of their two movements, much like the union Unitarians and Universalists accomplished in 1961.

Our Sunshine Rabbi was at the forefront of these forays into borderland territory. While serving a St. Louis, Missouri, synagogue in 1869, he wrote and delivered a series of lectures, "Reform Judaism and the Unitarian Church," that traced the two religions' similarities and points of divergence. The unity of God was vital to their shared theology.

That common philosophical underpinning manifested differently in each movement, however. Unitarians and Jews showed up at their respective worship services expecting different rituals; they would have to decide what would happen in a shared service. Would the liturgy be in Hebrew? What about communion, a standard Unitarian practice at the time? How would the preference for being called "Christian" or "Jewish" be handled? While acknowledging these practical points of disharmony, Sonneschein pointed out that underlying them were the parallel histories of Reform Judaism and Unitarianism. Each, he said, was fighting for "tolerance, freedom and the religion of humanity."

Drawing a map for religious unity, however, wasn't easy. Sonneschien still had concerns about substantive ideas and their symbols. Would Moses or Jesus emerge as the founding father (today we might say "parent") of a combined religion? Would Saturday or Sunday prevail as the day of rest? If the two faiths became one, would it cast its lot with persecuted Jews across the globe? After all, while two religious communities might debate and decide about altering customs and principles, Christian oppression against Jews would certainly rage on. The ugly truth was that the Unitarian movement of that day demonstrated no great urgency to oppose anti-Semitism.

Ultimately, Sonneschein would not turn away from the task of Jewish self-preservation. The dream of religious unity, he concluded, was merely that. The real task at hand was for Reform Jews and Unitarians to fulfill separately what he called their "inner missions." Reformers must disseminate the teachings of progress and reason to orthodox Jews. Unitarians must offer the same messages to conservative Christian networks. This talk about joint inner missions was not well received in Sonneschein's congregation or the wider Reform movement.

Personal tension brewed as well. Sonneschein may have been a radical visionary in the public realm, but his private life was in shambles. He was in a miserable and mutually unfaithful marriage, and he was an alcoholic. His struggles came to a head in 1886. When he arrived at a funeral, he discovered covered mirrors in the home of the deceased. These were symbols of mourning that he and other anti-ritual Reformers regarded as empty and backward. This might seem silly today, as covering the mirrors remains a common practice in the homes of grieving Jewish families. Even secular Jewish families like my own observe it. But to the Reformers, it was a potent symbol. The rabbi became enraged.

He was also drunk. After the funeral, in the living room of the bereaved family, he got into a fistfight with a congregant. The synagogue's president had to separate them (congregational presidency is not for the faint of heart!). When it was all over, Sonneschein offered his resignation and it was accepted.

Finding himself even more on the margins of Judaism, Sonneschein packed his suitcase. Before his departure became public in his own community, he had already headed to Boston and to the Unitarians. He preached at a Unitarian church there. In secret negotiations, he and leaders of the American Unitarian Association discussed the possibility of Sonneschein serving a Unitarian congregation.

Taking a Unitarian post was not as big a stretch for Sonneschein as one might think. For years, he had felt at home with Unitarians, in no small part because of his close friendship with William G. Eliot, pastor of Unitarian church of the Messiah in St. Louis. Sonneschein had preached there in the past, and at other Unitarian churches nearby. Philosophically, he had long admired Unitarianism's free intellectual tradition, lamenting that religious leadership in his own tradition was "too narrow" for his expansive worldview.

It's easy to imagine why a rabbi might have been attracted to Unitarianism in those days. The East Coast movement was embedded in US history, claiming as members many of the nation's founders and other patricians. Judaism, limited and suppressed by anti-Semitism, had less esteem and influence. Perhaps Sonneschein, tired of having non-Jews devalue his contributions, sought to create ties to help overcome this barrier. He may have longed for a strategy to lift up his people's deep truths for making the world better and hoped to build such a platform in the Unitarian tradition.

Ultimately, Unitarian leadership did not invite Rabbi Sonneschein to apply formally for a Unitarian congregation. I wish I knew why they discouraged—if not out-and-out rejected—him. I wish we could have a glimpse of their conversation or decision-making process. But Sonneschein's story doesn't appear in the UU canon; it peters out abruptly, curtailed before it properly begins.

Jewish scholarship, however, has been more interested. Benny Kraut, a well-known scholar of American Jewish history and Judaism, studied Sonneschein's life for the light it sheds on Jewish history. Kraut believed that had the rabbi been offered a Unitarian congregation, he would have accepted.

This history provides fertile ground for exploring Unitarian Universalist boundaries. Imagine if our movement had embraced a rabbi in the nineteenth century. We might draw lines between "us" and "them" differently now.

Would we have found it easier to support other unions? For example, might we have integrated gay and straight people earlier? Might we be doing more now to promote religious leadership by people of color? Would we foster more diverse theologies and rituals, or develop deeper interfaith alliances?

Few, if any, students of Unitarian Universalism pay attention to this piece of history. What does this tell us? It is a grave loss if we avoid religious pluralism because we are nervous about ambiguous borderlands as we construct our narratives and invite others to join us. My mother and father are not the only ones who bring more than one tradition to their partnership and children. Countless families, faiths, organizations, and governments take on the same struggle with varying degrees of success. Making sense of journeys like Rabbi Sonneschein's is a way to come to terms with religious intersections.

The Unitarians' decision not to invite the rabbi into our group can remind us to come to terms with other intersections as well. We need to get rid of rigid categories that bar people from one another. Each of us embodies a unique set of multiple identities. A colleague is differently abled, my partner multiracial. The kids in the laundromat where I'm typing this shout and joke in more than one language. My friend belongs to two countries, each in a different way (and can't admit it for fear of deportation). Folks in the congregation I serve are dual—zip code, dual—time zone snowbirds. I call myself queer because my desire stretches across the gender binary that tries to restrict attraction and identity to either masculine or feminine—but never neither or both.

Like Rabbi Solomon Hirsch Sonneschien—like my sister and me—we all come from a variety of marginal and/or conventional places. At its best, Unitarian Universalism recognizes these in-between territories as rich grounds for cultivating beautiful, unique identities. Far from threatening or compromising our integrity, this fullness of our selves is a blessing! It is the basis for forming strong communities (religious and otherwise) that serve and are served by our diversity. Nineteenth-century Unitarian minister and abolitionist Theodore Parker, who died shortly before Rabbi Sonneschein came to the United States, wrote of his hopes for our tradition, "Be ours a religion which, like sunshine, goes everywhere." The sun shines not to colonize, rendering everything homogenous, but to offer warmth so that everyone can grow and flourish. The Sunshine Rabbi lives among us as we traverse our borderlands.

◄○►

LEAH HART-LANDSBERG *grew up in the First Unitarian Church of Portland in Oregon. She graduated from Starr King School for the Ministry in Berkeley, California. As president of Unitarian Universalists for Jewish Awareness, she chaired the planning committee for Let Us Be Counted!, a gathering of UU Jews and their friends and allies in 2011. She now serves as one of the ministers of the Fox Valley Unitarian Universalist Fellowship in Appleton, Wisconsin.*

Roots Hold Me Close

Mark Belletini

Having a Catholic education—which always stressed the Jewishness of Jesus, demonstrated the Passover *Seder* so that we could understand our own bread-breaking, and sent us off to interview rabbis so we could know something of *their* tradition, I was not entirely ignorant of Judaism growing up. However, I personally never knew any Jewish people in my east-side Detroit neighborhood.

But my first Unitarian Universalist minister *did* claim his Jewish roots. Not only would he cook and lead the Seder every year; he also introduced me to a haunting style of Jewish music, the *niggun*, by using it in worship.

During my student days in Walnut Creek, California, a Jewish member of the congregation there invited me over for his family Seder.

"Jewish ritual is relaxed," Art said to me, and I've repeated that phrase every spring since. He taught me the art of leading such a ceremony myself, which I then did at The Starr King School for the Ministry, during a class I taught with Til Evans on food and religion.

When I began to delve into Unitarian and Universalist history, I realized that some of our Socinian ancestors, especially on the Eastern front, celebrated Passover 450 years ago. And that in North America, many Jewish congregations have shared interfaith services on Thanksgiving with our present congregations for decades.

But it wasn't till my best friend, Stephen Mistler (Stephen pronounced STEFF-in), approached his death that I finally got it. I finally glimpsed the depth of the Jewish tradition. Finally felt the Aramaic *Kaddish* in my bones as deeply as the Latin *requiem* of my own birth tradition.

It went this way. As Stephen suffered, I began to submerge myself in Jewish practices. You see, Stephen, his partner Richard, and I would sometimes attend *shul* on Fridays. When Stephen died, Rabbi Yoel generously opened the doors of Sha'ar Zahav to me to help create a memorial for my best friend. After we buried him, I attended shul more frequently, often with Richard. I soaked in the reliable prayers: *V'ahavta, Aleynu, Kaddish*; learned alternate melodies for *L'chah Dodi*; and marveled in the unmatched treasures of their local *siddur*.

But then there was the rabbi's *drash* (sermon) on Friday nights. Hearing the *akedah*, the chilling, impossible story of Avraham, a voice in his head telling him to kill his beloved son and wide-eyed Yitzak bound on a stone altar, is one thing. Hearing Rabbi Jane hold forth on that story was another. By paying astonishing attention to the text, she unwrapped the horror honestly, then sent it like a rocket into the sky with fireworks, completely transformed.

To accommodate crowds for the Days of Awe, Sha'ar Zahav used to rent the beautiful sanctuary of the First UU Society of San Francisco. That it was the church I myself first served was the gold on the lily. And on the gold, this filigree: The rabbi came up to me after one service, and said, "Look, we both know you are not technically Jewish, but you read at my installation, you come on Fridays with Richard faithfully, you contribute . . . it's time for you to wear more than a *kippah* at *Yom Kippur*. Time for you to get your own prayer shawl—a *tallit*."

Back when Stephen was dying of complications due to HIV, he was suffering more than anyone I have ever known. His partner Richard was part of Sha'ar Zahav then. And Stephen was moving toward Judaism himself at that time. And so we would often, all three of us, do *Shabbat* supper on Fridays, or share the spicebox for *Havdalah* on Saturdays, or attend services. When Stephen finally died, Rabbi Kahn came to the hospital, and then asked Richard and I to visit his office later that afternoon. At the office, he spoke to us of Jewish ritual mourning, the *shiva*, and details related to the upcoming burial at the Jewish cemetery in Colma.

But Richard started to rock a bit, as if something was pent up. Finally he burst: "Rabbi, Rabbi, I am going to ask you a question; I know you can't answer it, but I want you to answer it anyway. Where is Stephen now?"

Richard told the truth: It's not a question anyone can answer just like that. But it's a real question. I felt for the rabbi, but Yoel didn't panic. He did as rabbis have been doing for centuries, which is to answer a question *with* a question. He simply asked Richard, "Why, Richard, where was Stephen yesterday?"

Richard raised his brows at the question, but managed to say, "Why, at the hospital of course."

"And were you both at the hospital yesterday?"

"Why, yes, of course. Mark in the morning, me at night."

"What did you and Mark do at the hospital with Stephen?"

"I don't know what Mark did, but I stroked his arms and told him that we loved him."

"Me too," I agreed.

"Beautiful! Did you and Mark stay there all night?"

"No, we went to our homes to sleep for a while."

"And do you think your love for Stephen ebbed any just because you were miles away from him?"

"O no, Rabbi, not at all. If anything my love felt more intense." I nodded in agreement.

"Richard, in all of your years with Stephen, imagine a day when you were reading a book, and he was making a collage in the same room. Did you ever get up, leave your body, walk across the room, enter Stephen's body, and sit inside his skin, and say, "Oh, this is what Stephen is like for real, on the inside."

"Of course not, Rabbi; no one can do that."

"That's right, no one can do that. So you are telling me that in all your time with Stephen, you have only known and loved him from within your own skin, and within your own heart?"

"Well, yes, certainly."

"Well," he finished, "that's where Stephen still is, right now." And he tapped his own heart for emphasis.

I was moved to the point of paralysis. Richard stopped rocking. Our eyes were wet. The rabbi went on about the funeral. But I'm not sure I heard anything after that.

My experience with the deep richness of Judaism, in all its myriad forms, has an impact on my spiritual and intellectual life. I once officiated at a wedding with Sherwin Wine, the founder of Humanistic Judaism, and my best friend Richard now spends his Sabbath at the home of his local *Chabad* rabbi, cell phones off. Quite a distance between those two communities. *But both are Jewish.* And I have found wisdom in such rich Jewish diversity.

My present relationship with Judaism, now that I'm in Columbus, has been shaped by my experiences in San Francisco. That relationship looks like this:

1. I still celebrate *Pesach*, with great anticipation, every Spring here at First Church using a *haggadah* I mostly composed. I improvise the *Maggid* every time. Rabbi Litman congratulated me for doing such a thing. I celebrate the Days of Awe with a drash and a prayer engaging the themes of those great days.

2. If I read from the *Tanakh*, the commonly used word in synagogues to refer to the Hebrew Scriptures—or what Christians refer to as the Old Testament—I often use the Hebrew names of the books first. I often use the Hebrew pronunciation of names in familiar stories, as I did earlier with Avraham and Yitzak. I personally resist using the Christian interpretive phrase *Old Testament.* And if I read from one of the gospels, I still often opt to use a Jewish lens. For example, I never describe the "temple incident" as having anything to do with the son of Maryam having a temper tantrum because of the "cheating" money changers—which is just the old polemic about the "Jews and their money" written into the actual fabric of Christian textual interpretation.

3. I also never say that Christianity rose "out" of Temple Judaism, a common default understanding. I understand both Christianity and a Rabbinic Judaism coming to life at the exact same moment in history, the 66–70 CE war between Judea and Empire and the subsequent traumatic sack of Jerusalem's temple.

4. Whenever a local rabbi and I serve on some panel of "world religions" at Ohio State, where we are each asked to briefly explain our respective traditions, I always let him start. He says, "Judaism is not a biblical religion. It's a religion that uses the sacred texts, not as a quotable authority, but as a diving board into a deep pool of conversation, argument, and

engagement. The rabbis in the *Talmud* all disagreed
with each other, holding different opinions; yet all
of them were *in good standing within the tradition.*"

When it's my turn, I just grin, "Ditto, but with Unitarian and Universalist history instead of Jewish history." It's
a little joke, but it does tell the truth of the matter, at least
as I see it. I go on to tell the students something of our
history and practice. I tell them that I do not see Unitarian Universalism as a fixed set of beliefs shared by all but
as a willingness, like the Talmudic rabbi's, to enter into a
conversation about the religious questions of life, never
tip-toeing around the real differences that exist within
and among our congregations. I point out that the word
covenant, the word we most often lift up to explain why
we do things this way, was not invented by our Colonial
ancestors, but by Hebrew nomads thousands of years ago.
I explain that there is no such thing as a "Jewish-Christian
tradition." Unitarian Universalists share the riches of both
traditions—critically sometimes, unconsciously sometimes,
to be sure—but I maintain we would not be who we are in
the twenty-first century without *both* of these distinct sets
of traditions and practices.

Now, as I look over my whole life—the sensuality of
some of my Italian, but quite modernist, Catholic culture;
the broad and saving embrace of my Unitarian Universalist faithfulness to ever revealing truth; and the spiritually
deep experiences I've shared with my Jewish cousins—all

join hands together to keep me grounded and grateful in
my days as a Unitarian Universalist minister.

◄o►

MARK BELLETINI *is a Unitarian Universalist minister with
a master's degree from Starr King School for the Ministry and a
doctorate from Meadville Lombard Theological School. He has
served congregations in San Francisco and Hayward, California,
and now serves in Columbus, Ohio. He chaired the Hymnbook
Resources Commission for the Unitarian Universalist Association, sat on the Ministerial Fellowship Committee, and has published a book of meditational sequences for worship,* Sonata for
Voice and Silence, *published by Skinner House Books in 2008.*

THE DISCIPLINE OF FORGIVENESS

LIZ LERNER MACLAY

One of my favorite Jewish tales is one that is also deeply Unitarian Universalist—a story about the imperative to live our lives true to our (best) selves: Some Jewish scholars and rabbis were debating what happens after we die, and what that means about how we should live and what models to emulate. Rabbi Zusya, who was elderly and nearing the end of his life, said, "In the coming world, they will not ask me 'Why were you not Moses?' They will ask me, 'Why were you not *Zusya*?'"

I love that story. I return to it again and again to help me find my way, including the way I live my faith: Unitarian Universalist, influenced by my Jewish heritage.

My father was raised Orthodox Jewish. His Judaism was deeply cultural as well as religious. And the cultural heritage won out, since he left the faith as a teenager but never left his identity as a Jew. He handed it on to me and my sister. We were raised Unitarian Universalist and our whole family is still actively UU—and also partly and inescapably Jewish, which, thankfully, is fine for our Unitarian Universalist faith and congregations.

That Jewish-UU duality of my nature will always be active for me, both personally and congregationally, because I am an individual and a parish minister. Jewish theology and tradition have informed my personal vocation as a Unitarian Universalist minister and also now my congregation's life and traditions. This happens in myriad and still unfolding ways, but the one that's had the most impact on my life is forgiveness.

Jewish theology holds that forgiveness has to happen on the mortal plane, between individuals, before any larger (or divine) forgiveness can take place. This is a big deal because of the high holy days, beginning with the Jewish New Year (*Rosh Hashanah*) and ending with the Day of Atonement (*Yom Kippur*), when tradition holds that all people are judged by God as to whether they deserve another year written into the book of life. Forgiveness is required in order to be in good standing, pardoned, or absolved of guilt. Forgiveness is not optional, it's critical; your life literally depends on it.

Not surprisingly, this means there's a lot in Jewish tradition and practice about forgiveness. Perhaps the most important point according to the Jewish system is that *the onus to invoke forgiveness is on the wrongdoer, not the wronged*. The wrongdoer is the one responsible for winning any forgiveness that might follow on what they have done. The system is very explicit about what is owed and what must be done. These steps are non-negotiable:

- The wrongdoer does a bad thing, which hurts someone else. The person who has been hurt can just stay hurt. As far as forgiveness goes, they don't have to do anything. Which makes sense, because after all, they're the one who has been injured, and it's enough that they have to deal with that injury and whatever fallout it entails.
- It's up to the person who did the injury to
  - own up, admit what they did
  - apologize, and ask for forgiveness
  - offer to make it up to the injured person, however they can, however the injured person chooses.

Here's the crucial part. The wrongdoer must take all these steps with the actual person they hurt. It's not enough to process it oneself, resolve to make it up in ways we think make sense, or to talk it over with a therapist or other confessor. In Judaism, no absolution can take place unless the admission and atonement happen with the person who suffered the wrong. The human dimension of this model is so critical that ultimate forgiveness—the kind that gets people written into the book of life for another year every Jewish New Year—can't even *begin* to happen until we've made things right on the mortal plane with the person we've hurt. This is true no matter what; no matter how much we go to worship services or pray privately, no matter how many good deeds we do to atone or outweigh the wrong, there's no access to larger forgiveness.

Here's another kicker: We're not off the hook unless the person we've wronged says we are. In other words, if we wrong someone and go through the steps of admitting it to them, asking truly for their forgiveness, and asking to make it up to them somehow, they can say no. They can refuse to forgive us, and refuse to allow us to make it up to them.

At this point, things get complicated. According to Jewish law, this exchange goes back and forth three times. If forgiveness is still refused, then the rabbi can be brought in to help out. While the onus is on the wrongdoer to initiate this interaction, there is also some pressure on the one wronged to eventually forgive. Forgiveness is not just a whim, and not something we can just withhold if we're feeling grouchy. If we're going to withhold it, we need to take that very seriously and have a really good reason. This is not only about the relationship between two parties, or about the care and ethical treatment that human beings owe each other, it's also still about God. Divine forgiveness doesn't come into play—it just can't—unless obligations on the human level have been satisfied. If those obligations don't take place, the results are very tangible: One doesn't get written into the book of life at the next New Year. It's not about burning later in hell; the threat is much more immediate: You put your life here and now in jeopardy when you walk around with unforgiven wrongs attached to you. So we have to do our best to win forgiveness, but also the wronged person needs to try to rise to the occasion and forgive us when so much depends on their forgiveness.

These implications support the ethics of the system. The apology and the forgiveness have to be genuine in order to be meaningful—which enjoins the wrongdoer to really offer an authentic apology. On the receiving end, being authentically apologized to, and receiving offers to make it up to us, even if there's nothing more to be done, hopefully makes it more possible to accept the apology and find in our hearts the space and spirit of forgiveness.

Because of the Jewish High Holy Days' dependence on forgiveness and atonement, this interaction of the wrong-doer and the wronged is a particular tradition at that time of year. Along with other rituals enacted at home and at synagogue, Jewish people make a point of having conversations with their friends and family to clear the boards and make sure all is right with everyone, even if they're not aware of doing anything wrong.

Because this discipline of forgiveness has great appeal for me, I also practice it, and because the Unitarian Universalist new church year roughly coincides with the Jewish New Year, I find it a good time for my own atonement. I don't know how many UUs make these Rosh Hashanah/Yom Kippur phone calls, but I have done it for years. It's gotten so that if I call a loved one during that period of ten days between Rosh Hashanah and Yom Kippur, they'll just ask, "Is this *the* phone call?" Sometimes it is; sometimes it isn't.

Sometimes it becomes the phone call, even if originally I dialed for another reason, since it's hard to delay that sort of conversation once it's been suggested.

I've also preached on it and commended the practice to my congregation, and some of them have followed up on it. Because the atonement process shouldn't only be a Jewish, once-a-year conversation. The convention of an annual tradition only exists to make sure people don't enter the new year with blots on their souls' escutcheons. It serves as a sort of safety net, in case some hurt or wrong gets missed or ignored along the way. But this model of apology, forgiveness, and atonement is good year-round. It's a lesson in being a good person regardless of which end we're on. If we're the forgiver, it's good to be asked for forgiveness and to have some sense of obligation to forgive. And if we're the wrongdoer, it is far more fair that the burden to enjoin forgiveness lies with us. We should have to ask for another's pardon and to offer not only our confession but also our commitment to atone, because confession is not always enough to make things right.

Genesis says that God spoke the world into existence. God didn't use gestures, or ingredients; in the absence of everything but the ultimate void, the word was the creative foundation of all. Words have ontological power in Judaism; that power is an essential component of the Jewish model of forgiveness. This kind of speech has to be authentic. It has to be done right. If it is, its redemptive power is great. And if it is done wrong or inauthentically, its damning power is great, just as we feel a terrible burden when we hold onto accusation, blame, and condemnation.

There is a lesson and a power here for all of us. The accountability, relational nature, and intentionality of this system of forgiveness make it profoundly relevant for any people in any time. This is a human-based religious system of forgiveness. For those of us ultimately concerned with how we live in this world, that makes its ethical dimension very powerful. It is a theological system of right relations that says we are under obligation to those we've hurt.

On the other hand, we have the turn-the-other-cheek model of forgiveness. This counsels us to lift ourselves, if we have been wronged, above pettiness and retribution. This approach arguably diminishes the moral sense of individuals and of society at large by encouraging us to target the injured, holding them inexplicably accountable for unsolicited forgiveness or acceptance. To be unshriven is a bad state of affairs, but to be unforgiven surely ought to be worse. And it makes no moral sense for us to gratuitously excuse or forgive ourselves when we have not sought forgiveness from one we have wronged.

If we inform Unitarian Universalism with Jewish understanding of forgiveness we gain invaluable perspective. What does it mean to us as liberal people of faith if we say that we cannot live or act alone, accountable only to ourselves? It means living into our Principles: affirming and promoting the inherent worth and dignity of every person; justice, equity and compassion in human relations, respect for the interdependent web of all existence of which we are a part.

What do we gain when we believe that we hold each other's lives and futures in our hands? It means a more meaningful life. It means truer and deeper community is available to us all. It means living with greater closeness and honor with those we love. That's what it has meant for me. It makes me a better person and a better Unitarian Universalist.

＜◦＞

LIZ LERNER MACLAY *is a lifelong Unitarian Universalist, currently serving as senior minister of the Unitarian Universalist Church in Silver Spring, Maryland. A past two-term president of UUs for Jewish Awareness, she retains a commitment to supporting awareness of the gifts and wisdom Judaism offers each of us as individuals as well as Unitarian Universalist theology and practice.*

Holy Crap!
Counting Our Blessings

Liora Gubkin Malicdem

At the end of the sixth day, God reviews all creation—from the sun and moon to the earth and every living thing upon it—and determines that this new world is "very good." This world, our world, is a good place. The intended goodness of creation—earth and sky, beasts, plants, and human beings—is an important shared theological premise of Jews and Unitarian Universalists. Today, Jews of all theological affiliations draw on a rich tradition of this-worldly spirituality to live as a holy people, sacred beings, and participate in the act of *tikkun olam*, "repair of the world." A robust reservoir of Jewish ritual, especially through the practice of blessing, provides a *halakhah*, a "pathway," to acknowledge, recognize, and bring forth this goodness.

UUs share basic elements of this theology but not the practice. Unitarians and Universalists rejected Calvinist understandings of original sin and other Christian theologies that create a flesh and spirit dichotomy, denigrating the flesh and looking elsewhere for salvation. Instead, their salvific impulse focused on this world, recognizing the essential goodness of human beings and transforming our world through good works. Ritual, a critical dimension of religious experience, received less attention.

Unitarian Universalists inherit Protestant notions of the centrality of "the word" to faith and salvation, in contrast to the Catholic sacraments. This legacy lingers in contemporary UU suspicion of "rote" religious practice. UUs also tend to have an impoverished understanding of halakhah as "law," and so dismiss it as a coercive and deadening approach to religion that blocks direct religious experience. Here is where Jewish wisdom offers an important intervention. While the Unitarian Universalist Principles helpfully affirm direct encounter with the sacred, we diminish our Sources when we accept as a corollary that set religious practices are merely rote. Instead, I want to re-examine set practices, entertaining the possibility that they can encourage a direct encounter with the sacred, in its full range of manifestations. Jewish teachings on the relationship between *keva,* the fixed form of prayer, and *kavannah,* the intention one brings to prayer, provide an entry point for a halakhah—a pathway—for UU spiritual practice.

Traditional Jews live in a world filled with blessings. There is a blessing for everything. These include blessings for food—there are specific blessings for bread from the earth, fruit from the tree, fruit from the vine; blessings for

God's commandments; and blessings for reaching a joyous season. They also include less obvious and less routine, blessings, such as for moments when we see a rainbow or meet a king. There is even a blessing to say after one has successfully had a bowel movement. In the college course I teach on Judaism, my students often giggle when I share with them the post-poop blessing, but if you've ever had a serious case of constipation, you know that regular bowel movements are actually quite miraculous. The blessing reads,

> Blessed are You, HaShem, our G-d, King of the universe, who formed man with wisdom and created within him many openings and hollows. It is obvious and known before Your Throne of Glory that if one of them were to be ruptured or if one of them were to be blocked it would be impossible to survive and to stand before You (even for a short period of time). Blessed are You, HaShem, who heals all flesh and acts wondrously.

Once my students stop giggling, they often come to appreciate the earthy, embodied quality of the "sacred poop" blessing. It allows us to claim our bodies at their most base level as good, which is an important contrast to the body-spirit dualism of dominant Christian culture, a residue of the Calvinist theology we reject. Food, drink, rainbows, kings, bowel movements: each has a sacred dimension. For traditional Jews an encounter with each of these elements of our world, along with countless others, occasions a blessing that imbues all of life with holiness.

The blessings discussed thus far have a set form. They are to be recited at a particular time and in a particular way. Many begin with the phrase *Baruch atah Adonai, Elohainu Melech Ha-Olam*, often translated as *"Blessed are You, Lord our God, King of the universe."* Knowing the predetermined structure of the blessing provides several benefits. Imagine you see a rainbow. This is a spectacular gift of nature, and you may be filled with wonder. After all, the sun and rain need to align just right; you need to be in the location where the rainbow is visible; and you need to have the sense of sight to see it. Upon seeing the rainbow, you have a blessing at the ready to acknowledge this wonder-full moment. An encounter with a rainbow is, in the words of Unitarian Universalist Sources, "direct experience of that transcending mystery and wonder." Now, imagine you are about to eat a grilled cheese sandwich. This, too, is a spectacular gift from nature. The conditions of sun, rain, and soil need to be just right. Too much or too little of any of these, and the grain will not grow. In addition, the labor of many hands planted the seeds, tended the grain, harvested the crop, made the flour, kneaded the dough, baked the bread, and so on. We haven't even mentioned the cheese! Clearly, this sandwich, too, is astounding. Like the rainbow—perhaps even more so—the grilled cheese sandwich is worthy of blessing. The blessings for food encourage us to notice the sacredness in everyday life that might otherwise pass us by.

A set form does not preclude innovation. This is an especially important point for Unitarian Universalists, who might decide that blessings do not apply to their lives because they object to traditional God-language. Jewish blessing-makers who reject masculine, hierarchical, and even anthropomorphic understandings of God have recast the form of blessings in various ways. Some Jews retain the traditional Hebrew but use *Creator* or *Source of life and existence* rather than *King* in translation. Others make a slight change in the Hebrew, replacing the word *melech* (king) with *ruach* (spirit/life force). Poet and liturgist Marcia Falk's potent recasting of *Baruch atah Adonai, Elohainu Melech Ha-Olam* to *N'vareykh et eyn hachayim* ("Let us bless the source of life") infuses the act of blessing with radical divine immanence and a feminist theological commitment to human-divine interdependence.

Not only do set forms of blessing provide opportunities to acknowledge and notice the wonder all around us, they also help us bring forth goodness that is *in potentia*. Through the act of blessing, we co-create the sacred. The form (keva) provides us with the structure, the set acts, that embodies our intention (kavannah) and actualizes it in the world. Bringing together keva and kavannah allows us to experience the mystery and wonder of life. To benefit from this practice, we have to let go of the residues of an old polemic—that structured prayer stifles individual freedom to experience awe. Rather than block "direct experience of that transcending mystery and wonder," the practice of blessing directs our attention and intentions toward a pathway that, in the words of our first Source, "moves us to a renewal of the spirit and an openness to the forces that create and uphold life." Whenever we recognize that we are interdependent beings—that nothing we are and nothing we have comes from ourselves alone—we find an opportunity to deepen our spiritual practice.

Judaism is my birth tradition, and I was raised with these blessings. *Baruch Atah Adonai Eloheinu Ruach Ha-Olam* rolls off my tongue with ease. It is a gift of my heritage that can be called upon to notice, acknowledge, and co-create the sacred that is affirmed in my chosen tradition, Unitarian Universalism. How can the gift of this keva from the Jewish tradition be shared with Unitarian Universalists? I propose to begin with the congregations. Here's the good news: The blessing is one sentence! It could easily be incorporated into an existing component of UU liturgy or added to sanctify a current practice. The chalice lighting could include this blessing: "Blessed is the Source of Life, whose flame kindles our search for ever more freedom and love." A call to worship could begin like this: "Blessed is the Source of Life, who sanctifies time and space." A blessing could also be added to one of the most important of all UU rituals—coffee hour: "Blessed is the Source of Life, which nourishes body and soul." There is room for creativity here. As non-Jewish UUs hear the blessing in multiple settings, they could also draw upon it as a resource for daily spiritual practice.

In a famous passage from the *Talmud*, Rabbi Meir teaches that one is supposed to say one hundred blessings a day. This teaching reverberates in the lives of Jews from many different perspectives. In an online article for the orthodox *Hasidic* group *Chabad*, Rabbi Yisroel Cotlar suggests that achieving the goal of a hundred blessings a day is easy to do on weekdays; one need only fulfill the commandments to participate in the communal prayer service three times a day and recite blessings before and after meals. The multiple blessings in each prayer service, plus the additional blessings around meals add up to a hundred. Follow the form, and the intention takes care of itself because, when taking on these commandments, one walks in God's ways and serves God. Alex Greenbaum, a rabbi from the Conservative movement, considers the hundred daily blessings in a blog post, asking: How might our lives be different if we did this for just one day? He says that finding moments worthy of blessing is not hard; the challenge is deciding to notice the blessings all around us. The rabbis at Oceanside Jewish center in New York take a different approach in their online column "One prayer a day." They recommend that their readers begin with one prayer every day as an antidote for our tendency to "ignore moments in our lives without pausing to acknowledge and appreciate the world around us—for good and bad."

With the resources to acknowledge our world "*for good and bad*" Jewish blessings offer a second intervention into a liberal religious worldview that has often struggled to acknowledge the more difficult moments of human life. A minister friend of mine states the challenge in theological terms: People come to church because they are suffering, but UUs do not have a language to address suffering. Even as we notice and acknowledge the beauty and splendor in our lives, blessings can also help us to be more present to the full range of human experience. Upon hearing tragic news, such as the death of a loved one or the destruction of a synagogue, the traditional blessing is to bless God who is the "True Judge." This difficult blessing acknowledges that natural death and human evil are also part of God's good world. As people are overwhelmed by grief, the form of blessing provides a way to express what is beyond our understanding or what is unbearable.

Drawing on this traditional resource, liberal Jews are re-purposing blessings—using the forms of tradition—to bring intention to more mundane difficult life moments. A recent blog from "Rabbis without Borders" looks at how the traditional blessing one would recite after eating a snack, which blesses God who is the "Creator of many souls and their lacks," can be used to acknowledge that our incompleteness, our inability to be self-sufficient, our radical interdependence, is also part of this good world. Another suggestion for re-purposing a blessing—using the form for a new intention—focuses on the blessing "Thank you God for releasing me from this thing" and reciting it at the end of a messy divorce or the challenge of medical school. The weight of the blessing may speak more deeply to the complexity of having gone through a difficult experience rather than a sunny *Mazel Tov* or the *Shehecheyanu*: "Blessed are You, God, Creator of time and space, who has supported us, protected us, and brought us to this moment."

Unitarian Universalists can learn from this rich Jewish wisdom, in both its ancient and contemporary manifestations. We can develop a halakhah—a spiritual practice—to acknowledge and appreciate so much that is good in the world, and we can honor the reality that both the good and the bad, the gift of the bowel movement and the gift of the rainbow, the miracle of birth and the mystery of death, are part of our holy life in this complicated, incomplete, and wonderful world.

◄○►

LIORA GUBKIN MALICDEM *is a member of the Unitarian Universalist Fellowship of Kern County in Bakersfield, California, and student at Starr King School for the Ministry. She earned her Ph.D. in Religion and Social Ethics from the University of Southern California in a joint program with Hebrew Union College—Los Angeles. She is associate professor of religious studies at California State University, Bakersfield, where her primary area of research is Holocaust teaching and memory.*

THE MEZUZAH
AT THE THRESHOLD

NOACH DZMURA

Many of us don't adhere to just one theology. We mix and match them according to our spiritual needs, and we certainly don't systematize our theologies. We reach into the theological closet, grab what we need, and go.

When we study theology, or when we study to be religious leaders, spiritual caregivers, or religious change-agents, we still study one tradition at a time—as though they don't mix, as though we don't have interfaith marriages, as though we don't practice spiritual disciplines across lines of faith. We believe that theologies shouldn't mix, that they should remain inviolate and monolithic. This poisons all our theological endeavors. TransThe[ ]logy (the brackets in this alternative spelling allow space for "o," "a," or other more flexible forms of Divine gendering) suggests that the entire foundation of theological education and public worship should be rebuilt to suit the present-day encounter with theological difference that occurs in our *private* worship.

When we encounter difference in our personal lives, sometimes we turn away, but in many instances we move closer. When we marry someone who represents difference, we may change both our names and raise our children in one or both or many traditions. When we adopt a child who represents difference, we may teach our child about a cultural and religious heritage that may not be our own; because it is theirs, it becomes part of us. Our model of theological education should similarly embody a TransThe [ ]logical approach, employing both a unifying particularism and a transforming universalism.

We must build our theologies to suit the notion that we are religiously impure—and I mean that in the best possible sense. Americans have made an art form of mixing categories. Consider Jew-Bus (Jewish and Buddhist), Jew-UUs (Jewish and Unitarian Universalist), Su-Jews (Sufi and Jewish): Americans can be a happily hyphenated people. Every culture has its hyphenated people, and often hyphenation is taboo. But America has made hyphenated identities chic; we've commodified hyphenation. Rather than being taboo, our hybrid beliefs and practices define us. Our often-criticized penchant for picking and choosing from a smorgasbord of spiritual practices might be considered, in itself, a uniquely American way to practice religion. Our individual and family lives breach sacred categories and create new imagined spaces. There is no prophylactic that will prevent the sowing of our spiritual seed. The task of TransThe[ ]logy is to nurture that which grows in an intersectional spiritual landscape.

Progressive religious traditions have a unique opportunity to midwife whatever marvelous creations emerge from these furtive and fruitful theological pairings that occur in the thresholds of our sacred places. Progressive religions can position themselves as the *mezuzah* at the threshold, with the honor of blessing and naming and describing the theologies that emerge, and also with the task of connecting to new theologies and helping to sustain rather than colonize them. As we study how theologies interact with one another in the borderlands, we come to know this intersectional way of doing theology, and one day, we will be able to teach our leaders and our children TransThe[ ]logy, the boundary crosser's theology.

I was raised Byzantine Catholic, spent a decade as an agnostic, found spirituality again while living and working with gay men with HIV, discovered neo-paganism during grad school, and practiced an eclectic tradition for ten years. Then I stumbled almost by accident into a Unitarian Universalist church for the best social justice service ever (on the slave trade and the underground railway as it was specifically practiced in my home town) and signed the book to become a member shortly thereafter, without abandoning my neo-pagan tradition. After 9/11, I began to seriously study theology and peacemaking and contemplated becoming a Unitarian Universalist minister. My minister gave me a single task as he set me on my journey: "Find your own theology," he said. "To hold all the theologies that a UU congregation contains, you must have a very firm idea of where you stand." So before I left for the seminary in California, I began attending many different kinds of services. For several weeks before I left, I attended a queer synagogue in Pittsburgh and realized that I had found a theological home specifically in Queer Jewishness. When I arrived at Starr King School for the Ministry, I took a semester of coursework, and then switched to the Jewish Studies program and simultaneously began the process of converting to Judaism.

Even though I have found a theological home that fits me, there are many things I admire about Unitarian Universalism. It is uniquely placed to accomplish many things in the American religious landscape. I especially applaud Unitarian Universalism for moving toward an embrace of what Starr King School for the Ministry calls an "authentic multi-religiosity," which, rather than appropriating or watering down other religious traditions while creating shared sacred spaces, it celebrates those traditions at full strength within their original cultural context while enabling us to retain our own denominational identities.

Every once in a while, I get a hankering to revisit the tradition of my childhood, to hear the Divine Liturgy of St. John Chrysostom, to stand in front of a lavishly painted iconostasis, and to lose myself in contemplation of the divine on a waft of *piñon* incense rising from a gold-plated censer. As a Renewal Jew, I don't speak words I don't believe, and I go to church without inner conflict. To enjoy the Catholic ritual, I leave my head uncovered and remain Jewishly incognito. A visitor to the tradition, I am treated hospitably, but I do not reveal my Jewishness. Nor do I share this irregular practice with Jewish friends.

While I do not have any challenges with this in my personal theology, I am not okay with having to hide part of my personal history in my public life; nor am I okay with fearing mixing religions. This is not the way I would like my relationship to the Byzantine Catholic church to be, nor to the Jewish community. This is why I feel the need to invoke the deities we have forgotten—the Gods of the borderlands and the deities who change shape. I invoke them here to bring reality to a powerful image: I am standing in the front pew of a Byzantine Catholic church. My head is covered, I am wearing a rainbow *tallis* (prayer shawl) and my arm and head are wrapped in *tefillin* (leather boxes tied to head and arm that contain snippets of *Torah*).

I have done a lot of personal and professional work in the arena where Jewish identity, conversion, gender transition, and burial intersect. Based on this work, I teach a class called Elements of TransThe[ ]logy. All of this *meshugass* (Yiddish for "craziness") about theology between traditions probably occurs to me because it has been part of my spiritual journey to change from one sex to another. When you experience something such as a religious practice or a gender so fully that you to embody it, you never entirely leave it behind. In a hoped-for future, I *shukel* (sway) and *daven* (pray) the words of Catholic worship to pay my respects to the God whose divine son died and was reborn, to remember who I was for many years, and what the Divine was for me and my family—not to change my allegiance.

What is TransThe[ ]logy? The term can never be completely defined because it transforms itself as it encounters difference. Elements of TransThe[ ]logy emerge from the sacred conundrum of transgender embodiment. To be transgender is a conundrum because one becomes a kind of hybrid. The conundrum is sacred because intersectionality is the source and the endpoint of Divinity. All of us experience intersectionalities, and a the[ ]logy that maps out this new terrain is useful to all of us. If denominations are to take on the task of educating members and ministers and social justice workers for multi-religious life and learning, TransThe[ ]logy may help us to shape the curriculum. Some elements of TransThe[ ]logy include:

- *We are all* btzelem elohim—*in the divine image*.
- *God shape-shifts.* Shape-Shifter, Divine Androgyne, Changing One and Transsexual become names of God.
- *God lives in paradox, ambiguity, and doubt.* When we seek certainty, we're trying to nail something down. Since change is constant, there may be more value in holding multiple truths simultaneously.
- *Shape-shifting has consequences.* Just as a transgender

individual and her community, changing together, must bear the consequences of transition, a Divinity and Its faithful community change together and experience both the freedoms and the consequences of changing shape. When Allah and Adonai support the same community, or Christ and the Prophet Muhammed (peace be upon Him) . . . both the communities and the Divinities will respond to proximity with change.

- *God is one and many.* If God is a Shape-Shifter, They (a plural pronoun used by some transgender people to define a singular, gender-neutral person but here used as a Divine Name) can be Many. All of the Gods are true and real and must not be ignored when our paths move across Theirs. The Divine name *Elohim*, which uses the Hebrew masculine plural ending-*im* is properly translated as "many gods," but the rabbis instruct us to interpret the word as a singular deity. A plural Divine Being consisting of a universalizing one-ness and a lot of particularizing many-nesses, makes so much more sense when viewed through a TransThe[ ]logical lens.
- *God functions within and outside of your denomination.* There is a lack of theological guidance for people who live across and between traditional categories, a lack of theologies that work both inside existing traditions and in the lawless lands beyond—theologies that move a transgressor from abomination to

redemption by the talisman of intent. TransThe[ ] ology is an attempt to build a theological model that supports those who live hybrid lives.

- *Divinity is a social contract (and a social construct).* All our definitions are incomplete and imperfect, but we agree together, tacitly, to define God. The more comfortable we are with calling out the terms of those tacit agreements, and then negotiating and re-negotiating, the better.

- *God contains that which is unknown and may never be known.* The more comfortable we are with irresolvable ambiguity, the better. While ambiguity causes frustration and discomfort, learning to become comfortable with Divine ambiguity helps us to accept it in our communities.

Can we as individuals engage our hyphenated people from within a single theological "house" when they live at least part of the time outside of it? As religious leaders, can we knowledgeably and successfully minister to a person's multi-religious wholeness while we strive to retain a denomination-specific focus and gestalt? Does our denomination manage, without colonization, to dwell within the entire spiritual terrain of our membership? What does that look like, in theological terms, and how can we use our knowledge of that space to strengthen ourselves? Can we re-think denominational success to include the ultimate denouement of the denomination?

Non-creedal, multi-religious denominations are most suited to exploring and mapping out this place of theological silences and collisions that bubbles over with potential. While many people traverse these paths as practitioners, none have been theologians. In this frontier, we have to invent new theology that supports hybrid lives. TransThe[ ]logy provides an emerging model for those explorations.

A TransThe[ ]logian considers theological need at many levels—individual, family, neighborhood, community, denomination, religion—and negotiates the gaps to create hybrid or unique rituals that honor and uphold both tradition and transition. At their best, progressive religious traditions operate this way already. TransThe [ ]logy can render progressive religious traditions in the[ ]logical terms like no other theological approach or methodology.

With TransThe[ ]logy comes change and its consequences in community. Amid this change, one may begin to view the body, the community, the nation as a *mezuzah* at a threshold linking multiple realms. A threshold is an ancient location where many Gods encounter one another. I invite you to meditate in the threshold of your own denomination, and find what traditions and practices meet in that TransThe[ ]logical space, in you, from your own personal worship traditions. One need not pass through a single door: The threshold itself is sacred ground.

◄o►

NOACH DZMURA *was ordained as a community minister using the title Rav, by Rabbah Emily Aviva Kapor and participants of the Transgender Jewish Gathering held in Berkeley, California, in 2012. He served as adjunct faculty, director of educational technology, and executive assistant to the office of the provost at Starr King School for the Ministry. He currently serves as communications director for ALEPH: Alliance for Jewish Renewal.*

Do I Fit In?

Deb Cohen

Unitarian Universalism is a religion for people who, in the past, didn't fit in. Although some Unitarian Universalists were raised in the faith, most were not and came to it in hopes of a better fit. I sought that fit myself, as a Jew.

I was born in the early sixties to atheist parents who raised my sister and me in a Reform Jewish home. Our temple was beautiful. The "old building" was a mansion built by snake oil salesman Willis Sharpe Kilmer. The sanctuary was in the "new building" and had a screened-off room at the side where we could hear, but not see, the opera singers hired to perform at the High Holy Day services. In my early years, Judaism meant being different, having to go through the motions, despite my disbelief and my parents' disbelief, because That's What We Do. It meant cold, sterile services, where the only music was spirit-less, and (on the most special occasions) sung by paid musicians who didn't even know the Hebrew they were singing. I didn't fit in because I was a Jew, but I didn't fit in with the Jews either.

I don't fit in.

I'm not a Unitarian Universalist. I'm on the Board of Unitarian Universalists for Jewish Awareness. I'm active in our local UU congregation. I almost never miss my Chalice Circle meeting. But I've never signed the book. My hesitation arises out of my identity as a Jew. Sure, I know that my Judaism is totally compatible with Unitarian Universalism. Actually, my Judaism is probably more compatible with Unitarian Universalism than it is with Judaism; I'm one of those secular Jews for whom it's more of an identity than a religion. I grew up absorbing the implicit message made explicit in an old joke: There is only one God, not a Trinity —and we don't believe in him.

I've talked to a lot of people about whether I can sign the book and still be a Jew. I've found it somewhat comforting, as I've only consulted with people who are likely to say yes. And indeed, they've all said yes. My friend Jonathan says that, in the world's eyes, I'll always be a Jew. "Look at all the Jews who were persecuted even though they converted to another religion," he says. But I have the freedom, at least for now, to not care what the hate-mongers think of me. I care what the Jews think. I know there are plenty who would say I've renounced Judaism by becoming a Unitarian Universalist, who would tsk tsk me for my involvement. I don't want to care, but I do. I don't want to move to Israel and become a citizen, but I am comforted by knowing that I can because I'm a Jew.

I can't join a church. I won't. Churches are Christian, and I'm not. My UU congregation doesn't have the word *church* in its name. But it's still on the sign out front, and people refer to it as a church. I cringe when I hear that. I feel less included, much as I feel when I come across male pronouns used as the generic, or when people assume my spouse is male. As far as I can tell, most Jewish UUs are okay with their congregation being referred to as a church. But is that because the ones who can't live with it don't show up, or don't stay?

Do I fit in?

Unitarian Universalism and I were born in the same year. I've known about it since early childhood, as there was a UU congregation about two blocks from my house. Their sign out front had various sayings posted; they seemed pretty good to me, considering that it was a church. One time, the saying matched the one on my Dad's tea bag: "Minds are like parachutes. They only function when open." I went to this congregation, alone and trembling, to attend my first gay alliance meeting when I was fourteen. I went again many more times for the annual Cranberry Dulcimer gathering; at one of those gatherings, a musician referred to it as the Utilitarian Universalist Church. And indeed it is. After years of going to UU congregations for concerts, weddings, lectures, and square dances (especially square dances!), I started going for the Sunday services as well.

I didn't go for me. My partner wanted to go, but I resisted for years. I'm a Jew. I don't go to temple, or to synagogue, or to *shul*, and I sure as hell don't go to church. A couple of years ago, I finally relented, as we both agreed that she needed to be more active, to find more community, and that the UU congregation was an obvious way to do that.

Once there, I learned that although there's no common theology in Unitarian Universalism, everyone comes to address their spiritual needs. Well damn, I have no spiritual needs! I'm not a spiritual person (although various rabbis and ministers I've befriended over the years have expressed considerable confidence that I am incorrect about this). Still, non-spiritual atheism is no protection against the need to try to figure out the purpose of life. The best I've been able to come up with is that I'm here to enjoy myself and to make the world a better place. I have no proof of this, but do have considerable confidence; our nature, our programming, seems to point us in this direction.

I fit in.

Getting involved in our congregation has certainly facilitated my having a good time. I love the people, and the joys and sorrows, and the potlucks, and the people. I like the lectures a lot, especially in the summer when they're given by lots of different people. (I love the people.) I don't learn any less just because others insist on calling them sermons. And the music is fabulous. So much so that I hesitate to point it out in such a public way, as you may conclude that it's worth moving to Delaware for. But heck, I'll be honest, and if we have to build another wing, we'll do it. The very first time I went to a service they had a bluegrass band. I was so into the music I didn't even make it to the cookie table. So yes, our congregation can help me to enjoy myself, but so can lots of places.

And what about making the world a better place? That's *tikkun olam*. I have no memory of that Jewish concept from my years of temple and religious education. I do remember hearing my father say, "Let all who are hungry come and eat" at every *Seder*, yet I knew that my family wouldn't allow a needy stranger in the house. Neither would the Goldsteins, the Sternbergs, or even the rabbi's family, I was pretty sure. We sent money so trees could be planted in Israel, and left it at that. I don't know what other Jewish communities were like, or how things have changed since I was a kid. I do know that Unitarian Universalism is all about tikkun olam. Unitarian Universalists are tikkun olam mavens. Doesn't just about every UU congregation have a Tikkun Olam Committee? They call it social action, of course, but it's the same thing. I just took another look at the seven Principles to see how many relate to tikkun olam. If I counted correctly, the answer is seven.

But committees and principles don't heal the world. People do. I'm a psychologist, and I have been invited to accompany a lot of people in their quests to make things better. Although I am often overwhelmed at the complexity of human beings, I am growing more confident in a very simple hypothesis: Much of the psychological pain people experience is a consequence of not being oneself. Society needs us to differ from one another. We need people who get lost in books and people who are always on the move. We need people who take dangerous risks and people who are easily scared. We need people who must color inside the lines, and those who can't or won't. If we really want to heal the world, we need to allow and encourage each of us to be the best self we can be. All religions, including Judaism, encourage people to be good, and to do good. But Unitarian Universalism is unique in that it embraces our differences and trusts individual conscience above collective theology. It is a place of acceptance.

Yet acceptance doesn't heal the world. Change is about *not* accepting what is. I wrestle with this dialectic every time I sit with a client in therapy. She comes because she wants to change, yet I can't help her with that until I accept her. And she can't change until she accepts herself in the present moment. Psychologists describe the need to balance support and challenge. This balance allows the client to heal. The third Principle of Unitarian Universalism reads, in part, "Acceptance of one another and encouragement to spiritual growth." This allows UUs to heal the world.

I don't know if I'll ever sign the book. I do know that I'm seen and accepted within Unitarian Universalism. I belong. I fit in. With that acceptance, I am empowered to heal the world. With that acceptance, Unitarian Universalism challenges me to grow, to change, to heal.

—◦—

DEB COHEN *grew up in Binghamton, New York. She studied math at Bryn Mawr College and then moved on to become a psychologist. Currently she works in a college counseling center, helping students grow into themselves. She lives in Delaware with her partner and spouse Terry, where they are active non-members of the Unitarian Universalist Society of Mill Creek.*

100% Jewish, 100% UU

Sue Magidson

Question: What did the UU Jew receive in her Christmas stocking?

Answer: Her first *Chanukah menorah*.

There's a story there, of course. My parents were Jewish —raised Jewish and married at a synagogue. Over time, my literal-minded mother became uncomfortable chanting prayers she didn't believe in. My parents discovered Unitarian Universalism shortly before I was born, thrilled to find a religious home where they could be their true selves. They quickly became enthusiastic, dedicated lay leaders. Our weeks were filled with church meetings, potlucks, square dances, worship, and Sunday school. We joked that the family station wagon could find its own way to church.

Judaism took a backseat to Unitarian Universalism in our family—except in the kitchen. We were gastronomic Jews, eating *matzah* and macaroons, bagels and lox, gefilte fish, *hamantashen* and *kugel*. My parents never denied their

Jewish roots but chose to identify solely as UUs. The only Jewish holiday we celebrated was *Chanukah*.

My parents loved being UUs, though Unitarian Universalism's Christian trappings could be a challenge, particularly at Christmas time. My mother suffered through the words of Christmas carols ("O come, o come, Emmanuel, and ransom captive Israel"; "Christ the savior is born"). She thought long and hard about which Christmas traditions she felt comfortable bringing into our home. While there were always gifts by the fireplace on Christmas morning, it took several years before my mother introduced Christmas stockings and a few more before she decided that we could have a Christmas tree, provided certain conditions were met: homemade ornaments only, no angels, no tinsel, and many hours of stringing cranberry and popcorn garlands.

My first real taste of Jewish identity came from the movie musical *Fiddler on the Roof*, released when I was nine. I was captivated. Those were my Russian/Polish Jewish great-grandparents leaving their *shtetl*, taking only what they could carry, bound for a new life in America. I wore out the LP memorizing all the songs.

My curiosity about Judaism unfolded slowly over the decades. I attended my first Passover *Seder* in my early twenties, led by a Jewish UU lesbian friend who created an inclusive *haggadah* long before they were common. Grateful for her radical welcome and clear explanations, I fell in love with Passover. A few years later, I began happily leading Seders of my own.

In my thirties, I got curious about the Jewish High Holy Days. I loved the Jewish practice of welcoming the new year with reflection, regrets, amends, and recommitment, but the High Holy Days were synagogue holidays, quite daunting to an unsynagogued Jew. I'd visited a synagogue in seventh grade with my UU Sunday school class, but all I remembered was the pain of having my braces tightened earlier that day. It took me a while to get up the courage to attend a *Rosh Hashanah* service. When I did, I was miserable. I didn't know which page everyone was on, couldn't read Hebrew, didn't know any of the melodies, and was clueless about the rituals. Most heart-wrenching was the juxtaposition of insider and outsider. It was one thing to walk into a mosque or zendo expecting to be ignorant and uncomfortable, but these were my people and I felt like a fraud! Year after year, I wrestled with the High Holy Days, learning a little more each autumn. And then, at age forty, I was invited to work in Israel for eighteen months.

In some ways, Israel changed everything. While I felt like a fake Jew in the United States, in Israel I was Jewish without question. I met people whose great-grandparents could have been my great-grandparents' neighbors back in Russia and Poland—the only difference being the ships they got on when they fled for their lives. A Brazilian Jewish friend joked that, when his family escaped the pogroms in Eastern Europe, they got on a ship bound for "America"— but neglected to specify north or south. In some odd sense, our nationalities were accidental; what united us were our Jewish ancestors.

Joyfully I immersed myself in Jewish culture, amazed to be following a Jewish calendar. While December 25 was just an ordinary workday, *everything* stopped on *Yom Kippur*—no cars, no TV, no radio. I marveled at a society where liberal religion is almost non-existent—most Jewish Israelis are either Orthodox or secular, an all-or-nothing approach to religion. My Israeli friends were incredulous to learn that there was a middle way and I developed a newfound appreciation for Unitarian Universalism.

At the same time, it was challenging to practice Unitarian Universalism in Israel, with no other UUs nearby. While the Internet gave me access to UU newsletters and sermons, American Unitarian Universalism addressed a very different reality from the one I was living. This became most apparent in December, a rather bland, no-nonsense month in Israel. I was stunned to discover that nearly every UU newsletter column or sermon written for December touched on Christmas in one way or another. For an entire month, Unitarian Universalism felt irrelevant to my life. Further, the UU doctrine of love was surprisingly hard to stomach at the height of the second intifada, when fear was a daily companion. For the first time, I felt alienated from my beloved Unitarian Universalism.

Meanwhile, Israel was transforming my relationship with the Bible. I'd grown up as a Bible-illiterate UU, regarding Bible stories as fairy tales or myths—apocryphal stories whose value was purely metaphoric. Walking in the places where the stories were set—living those seasons, eating those foods—brought the stories to life for me in a powerful way. I'd spent time in Nazareth and Jerusalem. I'd swum in the Jordan River and the Kinneret (Sea of Galilee). I'd seen pillars of salt. I'd eaten fresh figs, dates, and pomegranates. I'd walked in the seemingly endless desert. I'd been to the site of the First and Second Temples. Suddenly, my reading of the stories was grounded in a physical reality.

My life in Israel was marked by great paradox. Amidst the ever-present anguish of "The Situation" (the Jewish Israeli euphemism for the multi-layered agony that is life in Israel/Palestine, an angst that every Israeli carries on a daily basis), I loved living in Israel. I loved learning Hebrew, observing Jewish holidays, experiencing many different interpretations of Judaism, and exploring Jewish history and the land of the Bible. I loved finally feeling Jewish.

Ironically, as my Judaism deepened, so did my call to UU ministry. Two years after returning from Israel, I began my studies at Starr King School for the Ministry in California. One of the great gifts of studying at Starr King was the opportunity to take classes at the nine seminaries on Holy Hill in Berkeley that comprise the Graduate Theological Union, learning with classmates of many religious backgrounds. One of the unexpected challenges was bumping into progressive Christianity.

Historically, Christianity and Judaism have a particularly fraught relationship. These two sibling religions went their separate ways long ago while continuing to share a common text (the Jewish Bible, or *Tanakh*, referred to as the

"Old Testament" by many Christians). Thanks to nearly two thousand years of persecution, torture, and execution at the hands of Christians, many Jews are wary of Christianity, even today. Some will not step foot in a church. Despite boundary-crossing efforts, there remains much misunderstanding and distrust on both sides.

The Christian students and faculty on Holy Hill were warm, welcoming, and well-meaning, but often clueless about the impact of their words and actions. Having lived their lives in the dominant culture of Christianity, they just didn't know that religious words like *prayer* or *Bible* take on different meanings in different religions. They'd forget to check the multi-religious calendar, scheduling important events on major Jewish holidays. When they quoted Jesus, they'd neglect to specify when they were really quoting Jesus quoting *Torah*, passing off tenets of Judaism as unique to Christianity. They vilified the Pharisees, not knowing that the Pharisees helped shape rabbinic (modern) Judaism. They dismissed the "Old Testament" as a crude precursor to the truth of the superior "New Testament," thus disdaining Judaism's holy texts. They didn't mean any harm. All of these practices are rooted deeply in Christian history and education. But to me, a newly aware Jew, these micro-aggressions rankled, hurting my body and soul.

Gradually, I was able to put words and theory to my visceral reactions. I learned an important new word—anti-Judaism. In contrast to anti-Semitism (prejudice, hostility, hatred, persecution, and violence directed toward Jews based on ethnicity, blood lines, and culture), anti-Judaism focuses on the religion of Judaism. It can be traced back to early Christians trying to distinguish themselves from Jews by claiming Christian beliefs and practices as superior. Anti-Judaism is theological (e.g., Christianity is the only true religion; Jews will go to hell; Jews killed Jesus). Anti-Judaism pits Jesus against Jews, overlooking the fact that Jesus was a Jew, engaged in intra-Jewish arguments about the practice of Judaism during the Roman occupation. Institutionalized by the Roman Empire in the fourth century, anti-Judaism runs so deep in Christianity that it's a challenge for even the most aware Christians to root it out.

While I grew to expect pangs of discomfort in my Christian classes, I was surprised to find myself bumping into anti-Judaism within UU history. It was painful to read William Ellery Channing's seminal sermon "Unitarian Christianity" (1819), in which he writes,

Our religion, we believe, lies chiefly in the New Testament. The dispensation of Moses, compared with that of Jesus, we consider as adapted to the childhood of the human race, a preparation for a nobler system, and chiefly useful now as serving to confirm and illustrate the Christian Scriptures.

Similarly, renowned Universalist minister Hosea Ballou's famous "Treatise of Atonement" (1805) describes the "apostasy of the Jews," who "fell from the spirit of the law, were lost in the wilderness of the letter, and therefore were blinded indeed." This was common Christian rhetoric of the time, but it still hurt my Jewish UU heart.

Ironically, Unitarian Universalism and Judaism share many theological foundations. Both religious traditions hold that there is a spark of the divine in everyone. Both focus on oneness and interconnection, on actions above words ("deeds, not creeds"), on life here on earth. Both have a deep commitment to social justice. While UU language is rarely offensive to Jews, Unitarian Universalism's Christian history and culture can be uncomfortable for Jews, as it was for my mother. For example, UUs usually meet on Sunday mornings, use a Protestant worship structure, and retain Christian trappings, such as robed choirs and clergy, organs, hymnals, and pews. Much of our language is Christian (*church*, *theology*, *minister*, *Reverend*, *salvation*, *good news*, *communion*, *mission*, to name just a few).

These cultural clashes can be bumpy for Jews, particularly since most UUs are unaware that they exist. One challenge is scheduling. I cannot tell you how many times UU organizations have scheduled major events on Rosh Hashanah or Yom Kippur, the two holiest days of the Jewish year. Too often, well-meaning UU congregations schedule their Passover Seders before or after Passover, as if eight days weren't enough to choose from. We UUs can forget that not all among us celebrate Christmas, oblivious to the particular misery of December for Jews. We use the word *unchurched* to refer to those who grew up without religion, oblivious to how offensive that might sound to someone who grew up Jewish or Muslim or Hindu before finding Unitarian Universalism. We have some learning to do in order to live out our intention of radical welcome.

Paradoxically, as I prepared for UU ministry, I found myself becoming more Jewish. I joined a Jewish Renewal congregation and started attending *Shabbat* services regularly. I observe Chanukah, Passover, and the High Holy Days, at minimum, and love adding *Tu B'Sishvat*, *Purim*, and *Shavuot* whenever I can. Renewal Judaism feeds my soul. It's participatory, egalitarian, radically welcoming, politically progressive, and it honors the world's religions. Services are joyful and soulful. At the end of an exhausting week, my spirit is renewed by Friday evening services, filled with music, chanting, dancing, and silence. I've grown to love revisiting the same Bible stories year after year with fresh framings and layers of meaning. My love of Judaism has deepened while my call to UU ministry remains clear.

During my final year of seminary, I realized with a start that I had become 100-percent UU and 100-percent Jewish. As a former middle school mathematics teacher, I know that this is arithmetically impossible, but in the mathematics of the heart it is deeply true. I'm not half-Jewish and half-UU. There is no choosing. Both religious traditions have shaped me in fundamental ways. Both traditions are necessary parts of my life today. I cannot be less than completely Jewish and completely UU. Indeed, part of my calling seems to be living openly at this intersection of religious traditions, with all of the gifts and challenges that entails.

I am grateful beyond measure that Judaism and Unitarian Universalism can co-exist in my life, with occasional bumps and bruises, but generally with appreciation and curiosity. My UU internship congregation embraced my Judaism, eager to learn. My beloved Jewish congregation blessed me at Shabbat services the night before my ordination, and my Jewish UU colleagues offered a Jewish blessing at my ordination. I am thankful that Unitarian Universalism makes room for all of me—including my Judaism—and I am honored to join the *minyan* of Jewish UU ministers.

—◦—

Sue Magidson *grew up in The Unitarian Church in Westport (Connecticut) where her two Jewish parents found a spiritual home. She is a community minister affiliated with the Unitarian Universalist Church of Berkeley and serves as spiritual care coordinator and chaplain at San Leandro Hospital. She is a member of Chochmat HaLev, a Jewish Renewal congregation in Berkeley, California. To her amazement, her favorite Jewish holiday is Yom Kippur.*

Counter-Oppressive
Earthkeeping

Ibrahim Abdurrahman Farajajé

Tikkun olam, especially as it pertains to counter-oppressive Earthkeeping, is deeply connected to and reflected in the heritage of Unitarian Universalism. A deep care for the abiding transformation of the world into a place of deeper justice for all parts of all beings is a guiding principle. Tikkun olam also calls us into ever-deepening relationship of care for the Earth and all of her networks. Yet this was not always clear to me.

When I was growing up in the San Francisco Bay Area in the 1950s and 1960s, I did not know that there were Unitarians (before they merged with the Universalists) who were not of Jewish origin. In fact, all of the Unitarians I knew were Jewish Unitarians. And all of those people were deeply engaged in the struggle for a world where justice, equality, peace, and love for all nurtured everyone. How could we live on an Earth for which we all cared deeply if we did not all care for each other? Little did I know at the time that my own life would be ever more profoundly shaped by growing in commitment to what I later came to know as the work of tikkun olam—the restoration, the healing of the world. But also, as I grew in this understanding, I would come to understand the complexities of meaning of those words and how they united the spiritual and political. The inside and the outside were inextricably bound up together: This is the secret of counter-oppressive Earthkeeping, a key element of Unitarian Universalism's Principles and practices.

Tikkun olam has played and continues to play a great role in Jewish life. There are many different explanations of the exact meanings of the term. The Hebrew trilateral root *t-k-n* of the first word is often translated as "fix," "repair," or "rectify," and also sometimes "establish." *Olam* can be translated as "world"; it also means "forever" or "for eternity" in the construction *l'olam*. According to Rabbi Jill Jacobs, there are four main currents in which tikkun olam can be interpreted. In her 2007 article, "The History of 'Tikkun Olam,'" in the journal *Zeek*, she writes,

From the *Aleynu* [a frequently-recited Jewish liturgical text] conception, our understanding of tikkun olam will include an emphasis on the elimination of evil and the restoration of the world to a perfected divine state.

- The midrashic [from *midrash*: a form of rabbinic literature that offers interpretation of Torah] emphasis on the physical maintenance of creation reminds us of the need to work to preserve the world at a time when human behavior is having a negative impact on global temperatures, hurricane systems, and other natural phenomena.

- The rabbinic understanding of tikkun olam as the creation of a workable social and religious system leads to a definition of tikkun olam as a mandate to correct the systems that make our own society dysfunctional.

- Finally, the Lurianic [the tradition of *Kabbalah*, Jewish mysticism, which is rooted in the teachings of Rabbi Isaac Luria] belief that individual actions can have a permanent effect on the cosmos offers hope that our efforts toward tikkun will succeed.

Seeing ourselves as part of a greater whole (or, in the language of the Unitarian Universalist Principles, part of the "the interdependent web of all existence") invites us to struggle to eliminate forms of evil that destroy the wholeness of the Earth and perpetuate structures of oppression. It urges us to keep engaging in spiritual work on ourselves. Counter-oppressive Earthkeeping means that we see the power in multiple and intersecting forms of oppression. Earthkeeping (caring for the healing of the Earth) demands that we counter intersecting forms of oppression, whatever and wherever they might be.

Today, we wait for outbreaks of peace throughout the universe. We wait for eruptions of peace and wholeness in our inner landscapes as well, for the one cannot happen without the other.

In the midst of climate change, the radical depletion of natural resources, the continued dumping of toxic waste in the places where brown and poor people live, the seizure of the Earth to build ever larger plantations for the Prison Industrial Complex, the work of tikkun olam calls all of us into ever-deepening reflection and action. This moment invites us to transcend apparent opposites, to see beyond ways of thinking that put spirituality and radical political action in opposition to each other, and to delve into the deeper unity that dwells in all and in which all things dwell. Tikkun olam helps us to experience how counter-oppressive work is not some dreary task of a political or ideological orthodoxy. Rather, it is the very work in which we all must engage so that all of us—two-legged, four-legged, winged, crawling, swimming, flying, minerals and all elements—might have life and have it more abundantly.

In the 1970s, African-American mystic, social critic, and musician Marvin Gaye, who was truly ahead of his time, wrote, "Where did all the blue skies go? Poison is the wind that blows from the North and South and East; Oil wasted on the ocean and upon our Seas; Fish full of Mercury . . . Radiation underground and in the sky." But he ends by singing the words (spelled alternately here out of respect), "My sweet L*rd . . . My L*rd . . . My sweet L*rd!" He ends with a prayer for the radical transformation of this tear in the heart of the cosmic fabric.

Sometimes people talk about different and oppositional meanings or understandings of tikkun olam as either just political or just spiritual, but in fact, the different meanings inform each other. Instead of two separate trees, they are trees whose thick branches completely overlap and whose deep roots completely intertwine.

Tikkun olam is the work of re-establishing balance and equilibrium. It is the work of creating resilient communities of thought, art, action, and devotion, where all of us can show up with all of who we are, in the fullness of our being, in holy boldness, celebrating the inherent worth and dignity of every human being, and of every plant, animal, and element of our galaxies.

Our work of tikkun olam is to radically re-unite the political and the spiritual. We can affirm the spiritual roots of counter-oppressive socially transformative work. And we can affirm that spiritual practice has in its roots counter-oppressive socially transformative work. Then we reach down into the depths of what can become alchemically transformative and apply it outward—in our individual lives, in our collective lives, and in the life of the Earth. Tikkun olam re-establishes equilibrium within our beings and in the universe.

We are in such crisis with the Earth today because of oppositional ways of thinking and being. We have chopped up the world into either/or paradigms, assigning more value to one part than to the other, while implying that it is impossible to be both/and. When we speak of "brain" and "heart" as though they do not need each other to work, we tear the fabric of our being. When we separate "body" from "spirit," we think of ourselves as something separate from the rest of life on Earth. When we divide genders into only male and female, with male being more important, and fail to embrace a gender identity or gender expression that goes beyond "either/or," then we do violence to the Earth. When we decide that certain skin colors or languages are more important than others, then we also do violence to the Earth. Often on the basis of such decisions, we treat the Earth where those people live as something unworthy of counter-oppressive Earth-keeping. When we decide that human heterosexuality is the way for the entire world, we also do violence to the Earth. This way of thinking can lead us to study plants and animals in ways that reinforce such views, and to do that is to do violence to the Earth. When we decide that only temporarily able-bodied bodies of certain shape and size are "okay" bodies, then we do violence to the Earth. When we only consider those with access to power and wealth to be valuable, then we do violence to the Earth, for this shapes how we treat the Earth differently in different places. And when we only consider humans to be important and not any other forms of being, that most definitely leads us to do violence to the Earth. How can we see Earth-keeping as part of tending to our own hearts and souls and bodies if we see ourselves in opposition to the Earth, and the Earth as something on which we must impose our wills?

But we are part of the very fabric of the Earth, the universe, and the galaxy-oceans of Being that flow within our veins, connecting us to all the other beings and to Being. Unfortunately, we have also often separated our conversations about what is going on with the Earth from our conversations about what is going on with our bodies. In the 1980s, when I was a doctoral student in Switzerland, I studied with Hiroshi Nozaki, a Japanese acupuncturist, nutritionist and eco-spirituality practitioner. In the early years of the HIV/AIDS pandemic, I asked him what we could do about it. In addition to the many things he suggested in terms of acupuncture, food, etc., he always ended by reminding me that the very immune system of the universe had been under attack for generations. What was happening to humans was not separate from what was happening to the Earth.

The core principles of Unitarian Universalism invite us to embrace the many-faceted dimensions and manifestations of tikkun olam in our work of counter-oppressive Earthkeeping. For we are constantly moving and healing within the interdependent web of all being.

Tikkun olam invites us to live the core principles of Unitarian Universalism in holistic and intersectional ways. It calls us to care for the resources of our Earth. Through counter-oppressive Earthkeeping, we can build diverse and resilient communities by caring for those resources and assuring fullness of life for all beings.

May we watch over the water; may we watch over the Earth, for from the Earth we have been blessed with the gift of life. May we, in the spirit of tikkun olam, guard and heal the Earth and learn from her wisdom, her cycles and seasons, her gifts, and from her initiations into the interdependent web of all Being. May we joyfully do the work of counter-oppressive Earthkeeping in the spirit of tikkun olam.

—◦—

IBRAHIM ABDURRAHMAN FARAJAJÉ *is provost and professor of cultural studies and Islamic studies at the Starr King School for the Ministry in Berkeley, California. In addition to his work as an Ajmeri Chishti Sufi pir (shaykh), he is also a member of the Chochmat haLev Jewish Renewal community in Berkeley, where he serves on the Chevra Kadisha (Burial Society) and is one of the meditation leaders.*

Picking Up the Pieces

David L. Helfer

I am a "Jewnitarian," a Jewish Unitarian Universalist. But that was not always so. For years, I fought against my Judaism, my birthright, unable to accept the G-d of the Hebrew Scriptures, a G-d who seems alternately loving, demanding, and completely out of control. That G-d sounded far too close to the craziness of the family I grew up in, where the parental responses were unpredictable and frequently harsh. So I turned away from any name by which a Jew might call to G-d.

Yet earlier this year, I found myself in a group reciting the prayer of the *Shema*, a central Jewish prayer. We said the prayer over and over again, until words became incantation and prayer became supplication. I was accompanied by a group of incredible people for an interfaith prayer vigil. Yet it was the presence of a close friend and Unitarian Universalist ministerial colleague that helped me translate this ecstatic experience into something I could share with my

Unitarian Universalist community. I trembled as I left this prayer circle, so open to G-d that I felt emptied and filled all at once. I turned to my friend, as we had been earlier discussing my eventual ordination as a UU minister, and said, "*That's* what I want at my ordination." She nodded, knowing that I needed to share with my UU community how Judaism can help heal us in ways that must be felt and can't really be explained.

The words of the Shema, taken from Deuteronomy 6:4–9, which were once objectionable and foreign to me, now rumble in the very depths of my soul:

> *Sh'ma Yis'ra'eil Adonai Eloheinu Adonai echad.*
> Hear, Israel, the Lord is our God, the Lord is One.

> *Barukh sheim k'vod malkhuto l'olam va'ed.*
> Blessed be the Name of His glorious kingdom for ever and ever.

> *V'ahav'ta eit Adonai Elohekha b'khol l'vav'kha uv'khol naf'sh'kha uv'khol m'odekha.*
> And you shall love the Lord your God with all your heart and with all your soul and with all your might.

> *V'hayu had'varim ha'eileh asher anokhi m'tzav'kha hayom al l'vavekha.*
> And these words that I command you today shall be in your heart.

V'shinan'tam l'vanekha v'dibar'ta bam
And you shall teach them diligently to your children, and you shall speak of them

b'shiv't'kha b'veitekha uv'lekh't'kha vaderekh uv'shakh'b'kha uv'kumekha.
when you sit at home, and when you walk along the way, and when you lie down and when you rise up.

Uk'shar'tam l'ot al yadekha v'hayu l'totafot bein einekha.
And you shall bind them as a sign on your hand, and they shall be for frontlets between your eyes.

Ukh'tav'tam al m'zuzot beitekha uvish'arekha.
And you shall write them on the doorposts of your house and on your gates.

But before I could be open to the experience of the prayers, and of the vigil described earlier, it was the offer of salvation, inherent in our Universalist tradition, that first helped me to reclaim the G-d of the Jews. Universalism's central claim—that we are all worthy, that we are all saved—helped provide me with a liberating theology, a way to reframe scripture so that I could see more clearly the hope in Judaism, the commitment to the world and to one's best self. Unitarian Universalism allowed me to connect the endurance and commitment of Judaism with the actions of our UU faith tradition—with the many ways that we work, week in and week out, to heal our broken world.

Of course, as a Jew, as one who questions, I don't accept even our Unitarian Universalist Principles and Sources at face value. This is good, as it is important to remember the struggle behind their content. At the time of the discussions between the Unitarians and the Universalists in the late 1950s, culminating in their consolidation in 1961, there was healthy discussion and lively debate about what traditions and ideas might best guide us. One of the most visceral sticking points—a disagreement that almost prevented a successful merger—was how much to include our Jewish and Christian roots in our Sources.

They ultimately agreed to recognize the Sources of Unitarian Universalism, which included, among other things, "Jewish and Christian teachings which call us to respond to God's love by loving our neighbors as ourselves." Unitarian Universalists, whether theist, humanist, atheist, pagan, or questioning, commit themselves to changing the world for the better. I want to take us back to our Jewish roots and make explicit how this ancient and still relevant religion positively informs who we are as Unitarian Universalists today.

Unitarian Universalist liturgy, rituals, and our very churches more closely reflect Christianity than Judaism. So it is easy to forget, or never know, the ways Judaism influences our Unitarian Universalist tradition. So let us lift up, then, the role of Judaism in forming and informing us as

Unitarian Universalists. Let us consider where and how the Hebrew Bible, that ancient Jewish call—often inaccurately called the Old Testament, suggesting that the "New" Christian testament supersedes the Hebrew Scriptures—brings us to our highest selves in the repair of our broken world.

I've watched and participated, for years now, in the lasting Unitarian Universalist commitment to creating positive social change. In ways too numerous to count, we are healing the world. Slowly and surely. The roots of such actions, come from many ancient faiths, but Judaism makes that call explicit. Judaism demands of its people no less than a full life commitment to healing the brokenness we find.

Such healing is known in the Jewish tradition as *tikkun olam*. *Tikkun* calls for the repair, or perfection. *Olam* simply means world. We are called to repair our world. In the *Mishnah* the first known commitment of Jewish oral tradition to the written form, tikkun olam is called for as a means to sustain social harmony, or said more positively, to work toward peace in the world. Tikkun olam is so central to Jewish thought that it is included in the *Aleynu*, the prayer said three times a day by observant Jews.

Tikkun olam does not inform my theology. It *is* my theology. For despite the complex theological arguments we can, and do, offer, it all comes down to healing the world—through unquestioning love, equity, and compassion. Whether our point of reference is Gandhi, Martin Luther King Jr., or Jonathan Sacks, a prominent rabbi who has called for economic reforms as part of the

Occupy movement, the messages are the same: Live your life fully, and in doing so, do all you can do leave the world a better place than you found it. That's it. Simple. Not easy. But a straightforward call.

Some history might help us understand the nature of this call. Holocaust survivor and teacher of Jewish mysticism Julia Corbett-Hemeyer tells of how the sixteenth-century *Kabbalist* rabbi Isaac Luria taught that G-d formed vessels of light to hold the Divine Light. But as G-d poured the Light into the vessels, the vessels broke into thousands of pieces because the Divine Light could not be contained. This is the meaning of tikkun olam: In healing the world we are metaphorically bringing back together the shards of Divine Light. Corbett-Hemeyer further explains how tikkun olam seems to reconcile the many unintended separations in our world—of gender, of homeland, of so much else. In a 2007 address to the UU Church of Muncie, Indiana, she said,

> There's a second aspect to the Kabbalistic story as well. Union between the masculine and feminine aspects of God is an important Kabbalistic symbol which predates and was incorporated into the . . . symbol of tikkun. The *Zohar*, widely considered the most important part of Kabbalah, holds that God's feminine aspect is exiled on earth as the *Shekhinah* and that she must be reunited with "The Holy One, Blessed Be He." We are called to participate in this re-unification of the holy itself as we repair the world. . . .

The metaphor of transition from exile to redemption is important in this story as well. The exile of Adam and Eve from the garden of Eden, the exile of the Jewish people in Egypt, Babylonia, and later throughout the world, were all understood by Luria and his followers as manifestations of a much larger cosmic process. Once the sparks have been gathered together, exile will end, not only the diaspora of the Jews from their homeland but the exile of human beings from the holy and from each other. . . .

Tikkun olam thus embodies the central ethical injunction of the Kabbalah: Humanity has been given the daunting responsibility to restore and repair a broken world. . . . It is only as a result of the world's restoration that both cosmos and the Holy can be said to be complete, and that humanity can once again be whole and united with the Holy.

Rev. Judith E. Wright explains this further in her 2011 address at the First Parish UU in Northborough, Massachusetts:

Then, with the advent of the Zohar, everything shifted. The new system of the Kabbalah that arose in thirteenth-century Spain held the verb *tikkun* as a central concept. Every human act has significance within this mystical system.

The world as we perceive with our senses is but a reflection of a higher, holy, sacred world. . . .

This was a significant shift: Hasidism removed tikkun from the . . . beliefs so that humans must no longer be concerned with the breaking and repair of broken divine vessels but rather with the correction of the human being within his or her own soul. . . .

Today, for many Jews, tikkun olam is viewed as a major commitment to their faith.

The relationship between God and humans is a covenantal one, where both parties are working to repair the world. [Today], to embrace this concept of tikkun olam is to go well beyond a secular response to suffering or chaos. . . . Classical Judaism depicts tikkun olam, or repairing the world, as expanding outward in concentric circles, in terms of aiding or helping to heal what is broken. . . . One needs first to heal the brokenness within one's self. Next, one can care for one's family, one's local community, then the Jewish community, and finally, all of creation.

Listen, deeply, then, to the ancient call of tikkun olam, the call to heal the brokenness in the world: Bringing about gender equality. Reconciling gender conflicts within ourselves. Aligning our beliefs and our actions. Ending our exile, from our homelands and from ourselves. Creating world community. Healing ourselves. Leading the way toward what is right and just. Reconnecting with the cosmos—the natural and the mystical. Each of these calls can be found within Unitarian Universalism, and within the notion of tikkun olam.

We must understand from where we come. When we feel burned out, wondering if our work is making the world a better place, where do we reach? How do we find the energy, the motivation, the passion to keep working? We can keep that shard of light—the reminder not only of our brokenness but of the potential for wholeness and repair—in our pocket, our hand, our heart . . . always. The connections we make with each other, the love that surpasses explanation, the endurance of community, the expansion of our hearts into that which serves others, all of that is tikkun olam. And Unitarian Universalism. It is the healing that saves us.

Our Unitarian Universalist Association understands this connection. More and more, I hear the phrase, "Nurture your spirit, heal our world." That is the call to which we must respond.

May we know our history and respond, again and again, to that ancient call. May we find connections between and among us—and in doing so, make the light of the world whole and bright once again.

—◦—

DAVID L. HELFER *is a lifelong Jew who found Unitarian Universalism seven years ago. He was raised in New York and now resides in Long Beach, California. He expects to be ordained to the UU ministry in 2014 and is also a proud transgender individual. He serves on the UU Funding Panel.*

EREV RAV, A MIXED MULTITUDE

KELLY WEISMAN ASPROOTH-JACKSON

My mother was baking cookies. I can see her leaning over to open the oven and check on them when I, an elementary school-aged child, asked, "Where do you think we go when we die?" And she replied, while those cookies baked, "What I believe is what some Jewish people believe—that we live on in the memory of the people who love us." This idea fit seamlessly in our religious community, the First Unitarian Church of Rochester, New York, where the inscription on the memorial garden wall where I used to play reads, "To Live in Hearts That Love Is Not to Die." It has served as a stable part of my theology, a gift from my mother throughout my life, even as many things about me have changed. It is also one early example of the way in which my upbringing taught me to see a profound closeness between Unitarian Universalism—the faith in which I was born and raised—and Judaism, the faith I joined as an adult.

Growing up Unitarian Universalist, I was very aware that most of the adults in the congregation had grown up in some other tradition. Some came from Roman Catholicism, like my mother. Some, like my father, from the various strands of Protestantism, then so ill-defined in my own understanding. And some from Judaism. While each of these groups sometimes joked or complained about their faiths of origin, at their best they brought the values, traditions, and art most precious to them from their original tradition into the life of the congregation that was now their spiritual home. So it was, for instance, that I grew up celebrating Passover at church, despite having no family connection to Judaism, because a leading member of our congregation was Jewish and wanted to share his family's practice with the rest of the community.

It wasn't until I reached adulthood that I came to appreciate just how relatively unusual I was—a Unitarian Universalist by upbringing who was still actively involved in congregational life. So much of our history compels us to be a religious movement with the gates wide open. Our roots in the once-Puritan congregations of New England draw upon the conflict between a narrow, rigid interpretation of covenantal belonging and a broader, more inclusive one. And our Universalist heritage reminds us of the illusory nature of human division: All people are united by a shared destiny. The welcoming, embracing nature of our theology, which comes into effect when we are at our best, has forged us into *erev rav*—a "mixed multitude"—the phrase used in Exodus to describe the community that left Egypt at the end of the plagues. Those fleeing were not only Hebrew slaves but also Egyptians and others who were connected to that group by bonds of family, marriage, or some other deep sense of kinship. Likewise, often the normative experience of Unitarian Universalism is a story of leaving one religious path behind and venturing on to our own.

In contemporary Judaism, of course, this is entirely reversed; the line between religion and ethnicity is somewhat blurry. Judaism's expectations for conversion are significant, requiring study, affirmation, and in the case of men, a notorious physical component, all of which must be confirmed by a rabbinic court. Judaism also has a taboo against proselytizing, built up over centuries in which governments and religious authorities persecuted and killed converts and those who assisted them. (Thus the tradition that one must ask and be refused three times before receiving instruction for conversion.) So it is no surprise that the assumption about most Jews is that they were born Jewish. (However, the assumption that all born Jews are *raised* Jewish is becoming less and less safe).

Despite the many ways in which, looking back, I recognize a foreshadowing of my eventual relationship with Judaism, I did not go looking for it or any other religious identity to supplement or supplant my Unitarian Universalism. Instead, the encounter arrived because I fell in love with a Jew. Part of loving someone is being curious about them and wanting to know more about who they are and what matters most to them. While that's hardly a unique perspective, Unitarian Universalism has taught me that love is a matter of mutuality—it changes the people it binds together, as each influences the other. When my love and I settled into our first apartment together, we became companions to each other's practice. On Saturdays we walked to temple together; on Sundays we walked in the opposite direction to church.

I began my life in the synagogue as a clumsy guest, acutely aware that I did not know anything: what to say, what to sing, when to stand, how to bow. Many of our UU religious education programs give our young people practice visiting other faith communities. That practice helps train them to be comfortable with the unfamiliar and respectfully curious about rituals and beliefs different from their own. So I began to muddle through. The tunes that accompanied the prayers helped me to memorize them long before I could understand them, and I tried to keep the most confident regulars in my line of sight so I could follow their rising and sitting. My wife was, of course, an invaluable guide.

If you attend a large enough Jewish congregation often enough, you will find yourself attending a lot of *bar* and *bat mitzvot* for teenagers you do not otherwise know. This is just a matter of math: Every practicing thirteen-year-old needs to lead the service and read from the *Torah* once, and there are only so many *Shabbatot* in a year on which to do so. Because of this, the sermons I first encountered in Judaism were mostly composed by middle schoolers, relating their lives and world to the words and stories of the Torah on the day it was being entrusted to them. I found it to be a wonderfully accessible and inviting introduction. There was also something familiar in it, reminding me of Unitarian Universalist Coming of Age programs, in which teenagers who are moving into adult membership often preach their personal theology to the congregation.

The centrality of the congregation in Unitarian Universalism gives us an ethic of joining and belonging that I believe to be one of our greatest strengths. However, it doesn't sink into all of us; in fact, much of our collective hand-wringing about numerical growth and member retention boils down to worrying that this ethic is deficient because not everyone seems to catch it the instant they walk in the door. We can and should be working to actively teach it rather than leaving it as a piece of our invisible curriculum. In fact, many of the congregations we consider "vital," "energetic," "prophetic," or otherwise "good" already are teaching this ethic. We might summarize the ethic this way: "If you are present, participate; if you are inspired, commit; and if you are disappointed, work to make it better."

It would have been easy to engage with Judaism as a long-term interloper. In many ways, Jews other than my partner and her immediate family would have known better what to make of me if I was content to be the non-Jewish spouse (and eventually parent) along for the ride in the synagogue. But my Unitarian Universalist ethic of belonging would not allow me to follow that course. I found in Judaism an ocean of stories, songs, histories, people, and practices that drew me in with a powerful force. The tradition also resonated deeply with the one I had been raised in, the one whose ministry I sought to enter.

There are any number of major points of sympathy between Judaism and Unitarian Universalism, but I will point to three:

- Both traditions are drawn from a diverse collection of voices, and their wisest and most courageous figures are still profoundly human and fallible.
- For each faith, what is most important in this life is how we treat ourselves and each other and the world entrusted to us, and what sort of society we build from it. It is the highest measure of holiness.
- Judaism and Unitarian Universalism both hold that we cannot become fully ourselves alone. We need community and relationship and the challenge and accountability that come with them in order to unfold the full potential of our lives.

The mystical school of Isaac Luria includes a tradition that the matter of creation contains sparks of divine light left over from the creation of the world. Prayer and spiritual practice, it is said, help to reunite these fragments with their original source. This is one of the ideas connected with the

Jewish theme of *tikkun olam*—the healing/repairing/perfect-
ing of the world. Tikkun olam is another Jewish idea I was
first exposed to in church, offered by the minister as an
elegant and poetic way of describing a value we also hold
as Unitarian Universalists, the spiritual imperative to bend
the universe toward justice.

My personal spin on Luria's vision is this: That which is
wrong is not necessarily wrong because the world contains
inherently bad people and bad things. It is instead a matter
of jumbled arrangement; things are not where they ought
to be. We are disconnected from each other, or connected
in ways that are harmful rather than healing. Healing the
world becomes a project of reorganization and reintegra-
tion. That is the lesson that I take from being a Unitarian
Universalist by birth and a Jew by choice. Because of my
experiences, I could not remain the first without also
becoming the second; to do otherwise would have meant
betraying the values I was raised with.

All of us Unitarian Universalists, of any theological
stripe, will find ourselves drawn to cross boundaries if we
remain in this movement long enough. As we do, we bind
up the disconnected fragments of ourselves and our world
into new and surprising wholeness. The lines we cross may
not all be religious, and sometimes we may feel tempted to
cross a boundary that should remain uncrossed for health
and safety. This is where the accountability of relationship
and community are most important, helping us to discern
risks that are prophetic from those that are reckless or self-

serving. It is in the nature of our multitude to mix, and it is through this action that we move toward perfection.

◄o►

KELLY WEISMAN ASPROOTH-JACKSON *is the minister of the First Parish Church Unitarian Universalist in Beverly, Massachusetts, where he has served since 2010. He is a life-long Unitarian Universalist and a 2007 graduate of Starr King School for the Ministry. He lives in Beverly with his partner Sara, their daughter Miriam and son Mordecai.*

A HOME FOR ALL SOULS

ALISON B. MILLER

I was raised in a church that has more Jewish members than many synagogues do. All Souls is a Unitarian Universalist church located in New York City; about a third of its members claim Judaism as a significant part of their religious identity and heritage. It was the ideal spiritual home for my interfaith family.

My parents arrived at All Souls for the first time when they were searching for a place to get married. They were engaged in the 1970s, when it was still controversial for a Protestant lawyer from Manhattan to marry a Jewish nurse from Brooklyn. The distance—social, economic, and religious—was considered too far to bridge.

The rabbis and ministers my parents spoke with refused to officiate at their wedding without serious concessions. They would require that either my father or my mother convert and promise to raise their children in that same faith. Having surmounted the hurdle of their respective families' deep disapproval, neither of my parents was about to allow another father figure to place such demands on them.

Little did they realize that the very traditional looking red brick church with a white steeple located only two blocks from my father's apartment held the answer they were seeking. After striking out so many times in more familiar territory, they finally came through the front gate of All Souls and met with the minister, Walter Kring. He greeted the fact of their engagement with celebration and understanding; more importantly, he told them that no conversion would be necessary.

All Souls became more than the location of my parents' wedding. They ultimately chose to join the congregation and to raise their children in the religious education program. They had found the answer that worked for our family. As my parents used to say, "We found a religion where we can worship together while holding different beliefs." Neither wanted to reject wholesale the religion of their upbringing, even if they didn't agree with everything it represented. Instead, they wanted to grow through sharing and learning from the wisdom their respective faiths had to offer.

My mother would often say, "Becoming a Unitarian Universalist has allowed me to become the kind of Jew that I am." She was a feminist born in the late 1930s to orthodox Jewish parents, for whom religious observance included observing prescribed gender roles. She was labeled the rebel in the family early on in life for doing things like interfering with the *mechitza* (the partition) between men and women in the sanctuary. She didn't think it was fair that her younger brother could be on the other side with her father and the rabbi, and she wanted to be able to see everything that was happening in the service. Her father was a well-respected kosher butcher in the neighborhood, with a deep commitment to the customs and traditions that had been handed down to him. Her questioning and non-conforming spirit continually placed a strain on their relationship. Ultimately, her parents ostracized her throughout her twenties and early thirties.

By the time I was born, my grandparents had softened in their views somewhat, at least enough for relationships to begin to repair. Even though my mother's very liberal way of honoring Judaism differed vastly from the approach of her more conservative parents, it was clear that beneath the particulars lay a common foundation. They all felt and acknowledged the presence of the holy in their lives, they had a lifelong passion to read and to learn about religion, and they appreciated the role of ritual and worship. They have passed these traits down from one generation to the next, and as a Unitarian Universalist minister, I consider these qualities as my most significant inheritance.

My earliest taste of the prayers, foods, and rituals that flavor Jewish religious life came on Friday nights, as our family frequently shared a weekly *Shabbat* meal with our upstairs neighbors, the Hoffmans. I remember the flickering lights and dancing shadows as we waved our hands by the candle flames, ushering in this sacred family time. I remember the melodies of the Hebrew chants as we gave thanks and praise for Shabbat, for the delicious *challah*, and the fruit of the vine. I remember feeling that nothing mattered more than learning how to savor that family time. In some ways, I felt jealous that my friend Miriam continued to celebrate that special time from that night on through the next day until sunset. Our family's religious observance didn't resume until Sunday morning, when my mother, father, brother, and I would go to the Unitarian Church of All Souls.

All Souls was the one place where the fullness of my mixed religious heritage seemed to fit in. In the world beyond, the uncertainty and the paradox that comes with a family blending two religions that sometimes contradict seemed to present an affront. It was not yet part of the norm.

I was the only child of an interfaith marriage in my whole grade and quite possibly the entire school. When fellow students asked my religion, I frequently responded, "Christian-Jewish Unitarian Universalist" or "Crewish Unitarian Universalist." As you may imagine, this led to quizzical looks, and often the following comment: "It isn't possible to be both Christian and Jewish." I expected this challenge to my label, especially from people for whom religion hinged on their answer to the question, Who is Jesus? I explained the Unitarian concept of Jesus as a great rabbi or prophet, as opposed to the Trinitarian assertion of Jesus' divinity, and described how elements of these two traditions could coexist in our faith. This additional information made some fellow students curious to know more; others responded by reinforcing the religious boxes that made them feel comfortable.

My mother was the first to "marry out" in the Kaplan family, and so we often bore the brunt of relatives learning to handle that boundary crossing. I recall an ugly exchange from my teen years, which occurred after my grandfather's passing. We were sitting *shiva* in his apartment, and I wanted to honor his memory by understanding and following all of the customs that he cherished. I asked my aunt about the meaning of covering the mirrors and other practices. Her quick response added to my grief: "If you don't know what to do and how to behave, then maybe you don't belong here." She went on grumbling in a low voice about how my mother hadn't raised us right.

In the open-hearted and open-minded setting of Unitarian Universalism, I felt the absence of judgment. In that sacred space, my family was viewed as doubly blessed by an authentic link to two rich traditions. Plus, we were not alone. The numbers of interfaith couples, including those with children, continued to rise. By the 1980s, there were enough members with Jewish leanings that a study and practice group called Unitarian Universalists for Jewish Awareness (UUJA) was born. My mother became heavily involved, and this led to a renewal of my family's connection to our Jewish roots. While we had observed certain elements of Judaism and Jewish culture at home, we were now connected to a larger religious community that sought to incorporate insights and practices from Jewish holidays, ethics, and theology.

The calendar at All Souls began to change. Sunday services and religious education classes included themes from the Jewish liturgical year, and additional services were added beyond Sunday morning. This story of the influence of Judaism in Unitarian Universalism was also unfolding outside of New York City. The congregation I now serve as minister, the Morristown Unitarian Fellowship in New Jersey, was experiencing similar developments. This makes sense because the Morristown congregation also draws a third of its members from one of the branches of Judaism.

These vibrant pockets, where so many have a direct connection to Judaism are fairly unique. When I served as an intern minister at All Souls Church in Tulsa, I could count on one hand the number of us with Jewish roots. People were very interested in my background as a lifelong Unitarian Universalist and a "half-Jew," as we are often called. I was asked to teach a class on Judaism, which gave me an opportunity to bring to life the smells and sights and sounds of holidays I celebrated with family and with All Souls in New York. It also allowed me to reflect on and share what I learned in Hebrew classes and Judaism classes at divinity school. Later in the spring, I co-led a community-wide Passover *Seder*. It warmed my heart that so many showed up to participate and to embody our UU belief in learning from the wisdom of the world religions.

I have to admit, though, celebrating the Seder in a space where most present had never tasted the foods or retold the story before was so different from what I had grown accustomed to in my home congregation and also in the congregation I now serve.

Almost every year, I have paid attention to the rhythm of the Jewish year. I have attended, taken an active supporting role, or been the leader of an *Erev Rosh Hashanah* service, an *Erev Yom Kippur* service, and a Passover Seder at a Unitarian Universalist congregation for as long as I can remember. The memories of these experiences are woven into the fabric of my faith as it has been lived out— . . . chopping apples in the kitchen for Rosh Hashanah and again for the *charoset* recipe at Passover; . . . the beauty of the kindled festival lights alongside of our flaming chalice; . . . the sharp and haunting sound of the *shofar* calling me to pay attention, to turn inward, to examine my life and to do better; . . . the times we have invited an Israeli folk dance teacher and sought to relive the joyful experience of Miriam leading her people in a dance following their narrow escape across the Red Sea; . . . the opportunity to rededicate ourselves to principles shared by Judaism and Unitarian Universalism, including our work of liberation, love, and healing our broken world.

At their best, the liturgies of these services strike a meaningful balance between tradition and innovation. On one hand, we have the opportunity to share in the prayers, blessings, themes, music, and foods and fasts that have nourished our Jewish ancestors for thousands of years. On the other hand, the gathering includes people without Jewish heritage and Jews who draw from sources outside of Judaism for wisdom and inspiration. The traditional liturgies need to be carefully updated and adapted to fit the context of the particular UU congregation, and the community's familiarity with the holiday being honored and its underlying themes. It is important to cover certain territory, such as why we as Unitarian Universalists are celebrating a Jewish holiday, and to link it to our religious values. Explanations also need to be included for individuals visiting the service for the first time. In addition, it is important to acknowledge the difference between our religious home and an Orthodox, Conservative, Reform, Reconstructionist or humanistic Jewish community where the entire Jewish liturgical year will be celebrated. For example, the solemnity of Yom Kippur is balanced by the great joy of *Sukkot*, which immediately follows in the calendar. Yet, despite this limitation, the Jewish rituals and themes that we choose to honor can transform our members. When certain holidays become truly integrated into the life of a congregation, many members return year after year, and gain a deep and nuanced understanding of what the holiday has to offer for our religious journey.

When we create an environment like this, we convey a message: Even though Unitarian Universalism is not a traditional Jewish setting, we include Jewish teachings as a source of truth and meaning, and we are enriched by this strand of faith and its accompanying ethics, wisdom, and set of rituals.

I have found the creative synergies and tensions that arise as I honor my half-Jewish taproot, while also identifying as a lifelong Unitarian Universalist, to be absolutely enriching to my religious journey.

◄○►

ALISON B. MILLER *is a lifelong Unitarian Universalist who was born into an interfaith Jewish-Protestant family. She was raised in and later served at All Souls in New York City, and now serves the Morristown Unitarian Fellowship, both of which are congregations with significant Jewish UU populations. She has celebrated the Jewish holidays in a Unitarian Universalist context throughout her life.*

A DAUGHTER'S QUEST FOR
IDENTITY THROUGH FOOD

HANNAH ELLER-ISAACS

"What is a *matzah* ball?" a non-Jewish friend may ask. Or the all-too-common, "Why not just eat chicken noodle?" This simple, delicious ball of matzah meal may be my first real connection to my Jewish heritage. I knew from a young age that my father had been raised Jewish and that therefore I was only "Jew . . . ish." I also knew in the depths of my soul that matzah ball soup, *challah*, and *latkes* were a part of me. These traditional foods connected me to my heritage. Like most children, I did not fully understand this connection, yet it was part of a deeper need for connection to community, to family, to my own history. Being raised by two Unitarian Universalist minister parents, I spent many years in UU religious education classes. I especially remember the "Neighboring Churches" curriculum, with its field trip to a Bay Area temple. I had a visceral connection to the Hebrew I heard spoken there and the words of the *Torah*. My connection to my Jewish heritage would continue to develop and deepen as I grew older.

In Oakland, California, sixth grade is the year you learn more about World War II and the *Shoah*. I became fascinated with D-day and its American heroes and French Resistance workers. I gobbled up the stories of survivors and victims of the Shoah. I realized that my love of Jewish food was part of something much deeper. Hitler and the Nazi party would have considered me a Jew. They would not have cared that this identity came to me via my father—not my mother, as Jews traditionally trace Judaism.

It became more important to me to define my cultural identity in terms of my father's side of the family—the Isaacs. I related more strongly to the Jewish side of my ancestry partly because I was raised by a vivacious, independent, and, let's be honest, outspoken woman. My mother had a strong hand in the way I was raised and I will always love her for her honesty. And as fate would have it, she also possessed the ability to channel a stereotypical Jewish mother. I was drawn to studying the Shoah for many reasons but the most important is that I saw myself, my family, and my ancestors in the faces of the families being sent to almost certain doom. I saw them also in the faces in the survivors, who reclaimed their humanity after the war by continuing to complete the simple, everyday tasks that had been denied them for so long. In his memoir, *Survival at Auschwitz*, Primo Levi writes,

All took leave from life in the manner which most suited them. Some praying, some deliberately drunk, others lustfully intoxicated for the first time. But the mothers stayed up to prepare food for the journey with tender care, and washed their children and packed the luggage; and at dawn the barbed wire was full of children's washing hung out in the wind to dry. Nor did they forget the diapers, the toys, the cushions and the hundred other small things which mothers remember and which children always need.

In her essay "Food Talk: Gendered Responses to the Holocaust," Myrna Goldenberg describes the ways prisoners of the concentration camps kept their humanity alive and honored the memories of the millions of deceased through keeping their recipes alive. Food has always played an important role in the process of cultural identification. Many Shoah narratives are shaped by the writers' memories of their physical needs and feelings.

Food also presents an opportunity for normalcy. In *The Diary of Mary Berg,* the author remembers a birthday in the ghetto when her mother had saved months of sugar rations to try to bake a proper birthday cake. For Jewish people, cooking and caring for their families is a religious commandment set forth by G-d and passed down from generation to generation. For example, women are ordered to bake *challah* every Friday and maintain Sabbath commandments. Of course, given the conditions of the Shoah, no one could completely maintain their traditions, but they did the best they could to conserve their traditions and faith. In doing so, they sought to cement their sense of community and individual humanity in the face of terror.

Food had always played an important role in our family life. Family dinners continue to be an important part of our family identity. Perhaps this is why my memories are always shaped by what I ate on a particular trip. In the sixth grade—the most intense period of my curiosity about the Shoah before college—my class was given the task of putting together a potluck of culturally inspired dishes that reflected our heritage. When I got home, I knew right away which side of the family I should cook from. Although I knew much more about my maternal grandmother's cooking and cultural heritage, I wanted to bring something identifiably Jewish. There are many different ways to consider what it means to cook a Jewish dish. I realized immediately that my father and his family had not eaten traditional fare, with the exception of holidays and times at Grandmother Isaacs's house. My father tells the story of going out to eat with his father, whose favorite salad was iceberg lettuce with bacon crumbles—hardly a Kosher meal. In the end, my dad and I decided that we would make sweet *kugel*, my great-grandmother's recipe. It was left mostly untouched by my classmates. Sweet noodles proved to be a little too much for my classmates, who felt more comfortable trying our teacher's Iowan Jello "salad" with cool whip and cottage cheese.

As interested as I was in the "food of my people," I knew very little about it beyond the importance of properly formed matzah balls and crispy *latkes*. Recently, my aunt compiled a collection of family recipes for my siblings and me. The details of some of them have been lost over the years, but the stories behind them continue to captivate me. It is clear that, for my family as for all people, food has played an important part in our history and cultural development. The recipes include Cabbage and Noodles, Sweet and Sour Cabbage, Al's Kivied Eggs (one of the few dishes my grandfather could cook), Fried Smelt, Matzah Ball Soup (secret family recipe), and Silka's Dilly Beans. One of the memories that my dad and aunt share is attending *Seders* for *Pesach* (Passover) at David and Silka Cohen's house. We still make Silka's Dilly Beans to this day, and each time we make them, I remember the history of my family and the relationships that have formed my cultural identity.

In Jewish tradition, when someone dies, they not only leave this world different than it was before but they also have a hand in shaping the next one. It is said that when a new baby is going to be born all their ancestors give it the traits it will have before it even leaves the womb. Cooking the recipes of my family makes me feel as though I am still connecting with some of them and learning something from their lives, even those who have been gone for years. Because of this concrete connection, I continue to feel grounded in Judaism through my family and my cultural identity. I am grateful that I was raised in a faith community that allowed me to build my own spiritual and cultural identity.

As I become more theologically grounded in Judaism, I also increasingly appreciate the role Unitarian Universalism has played in the history of religious freedom. I will always feel somewhere in between Judaism and Unitarian Universalism. I feel fortunate to live in a culture and family that not only encourages but supports this sense of questioning. It has been difficult for me to feel grounded in Unitarian Universalism as a spiritual home because the church has always been my parents' place of business. On "Take Your Daughter to Work Day," I would go to church. Yet I feel incredibly blessed that my parents have been able to follow their calling and know that they are excellent ministers. I know that, as I continue to develop my faith and my cultural identity, I will have the support of my family and community.

‑‑◦‑‑

HANNAH ELLER-ISAACS *is a recent graduate of the University of Minnesota with a BA in Religious Studies and a minor in Jewish Studies. She was raised by two Unitarian Universalist ministers and served on both the Youth Council and Steering Committee of Young Religious Unitarian Universalists. Raised Unitarian Universalist since birth, Hannah has always been interested in connecting to her Jewish heritage.*

Welcomed Guest or Family?

Rick Fierberg

This essay is for the leaders and thought shapers in Unitarian Universalism who claim "radical hospitality," who champion the oppressed or marginalized, and who promote programs that extend a warm welcome to peoples whose sexual orientation, skin color, or socioeconomic or cultural background cause them to feel excluded. It is also for my friends and family, who have witnessed my embrace of Unitarian Universalism and sometimes asked me questions that I cannot easily answer.

I have been a Unitarian Universalist for over a dozen years. Before I became a UU, I've had limited institutional affiliations. I have much more in common with the millions of Americans who identify their religion as "none" than with the approximately 217,000 Unitarian Universalists in the United States. I have probably participated in more than half of the many membership and service opportunities available in my sizable and prominent UU community. I have participated in local and regional social action programs beyond the congregation, contributed membership dues to the UU Service Committee and UU United Nations Office, and recently completed six years of service to my UU District Board of Trustees. Within my home congregation, I have found and fostered a community that has given me meaningful avenues for worship, prayer, meditation, and good works. I have formed rich and meaningful friendships, and created a network that further delights me through unexpected casual encounters while I'm out and about in the public sphere. In a word, I belong.

During worship services, I have learned moral and spiritual teachings from many of the world's great paths and religions, celebrated aspirations and fulfillment of the human spirit, experienced the majesty of great poetry, embraced nature as a teacher of universal truths, and lifted my voice in inspirational song alongside those of similar and different backgrounds and beliefs. With fellow UUs, I have shared meals and chores, ideas and artistic expressions, joys and concerns. I've walked labyrinths, square danced, played Wiffle Ball, practiced yoga, attended live performances, and watched election returns, Oscars, and the Super Bowl. When I realized that I sometimes raided the refrigerator and had unclogged the toilet at the congregation, I could clearly see I had found my home.

I've connected with myself and others, not only on Sunday morning but also throughout the week with committee work and lifespan educational programs, at springtime retreats, and via social media postings, where roughly half my Facebook friends are UUs. When my small group ministry gathering meets to discuss its monthly topic, I bear intimate witness to lives filled with deep wonder and the full range of emotions that accompany family crises, life transitions, disease, and death.

I've visited more than two dozen other UU congregations, and I accompanied the Transylvanian partner church visitors to New York City. In addition, through my home congregation, I worked with a local farm to help them create a CSA (community-supported agriculture) food program that began within the congregation and now feeds several hundred additional families each year.

Within a year of joining my local congregation, I began teaching religious education, from kindergarten through middle school. After facilitating the Coming of Age credo program one year, I was asked to share my own "This I Believe" statement at a lay-led summer worship service. I have also teamed with others to present worship services dedicated to the joys of summer and the spirituality of baseball.

You might think that such a broad, deep, and rewarding array of connections would make me into a walking, talking, evangelical enthusiast for Unitarian Universalism. I am not.

Beginning in the spring of 2009, the UU Metro New York District Board brought antiracism, anti-oppression, and multiculturalism to the forefront of its agenda. Once

I began hearing discussions about race and sexual orientation attached to deep welcoming and intentionality, it became impossible for me to ignore my perception that this welcome did *not* extend to those with non-Christian backgrounds. I began to speak up about this, uneasily, and *always* felt like I was at risk of dissipating a decade of accumulated social capital.

As a white, heterosexual, middle-class, male UU, I could "pass" as a Mary Oliver-quoting, micro-financing, spiritual descendant of the nineteenth-century Transcendentalists. And my parents had raised me to be a "nice Jewish boy" who would reflect well on the community from which I came. So I agonized over whether I should avoid making waves, or whether I'd been called upon to do something more. Was there a contribution I could make on behalf of others with my story? And could I contribute something beyond the contours of my story, one that might increase the welcome felt by those with a variety of perspectives?

After an all-day conference with Rev. Mark Morrison-Reed in December 2009—in which he led us through Unitarian Universalism's African-American history—I knew that I would have to ground myself in personal experience. On the following day, when Morrison-Reed was a guest in my congregation's pulpit, I sang a *Chanukah* blessing, a capella, during the candle-lighting portion of the service. I introduced it as the only song I had ever been taught by and sung with my parents. My candle was the lone recognition of the Jewish festival of lights that year in a worship service.

The following several weeks were reserved for Christmas, a beautiful holiday that is as culturally significant for those of Christian backgrounds as Chanukah is for those of Jewish backgrounds. For children and parents of intermarried Jewish-Christian members of UU congregations, this is no small matter.

Despite reading and hearing statistical claims that UUs do not primarily identify as Christian, I have come to believe that the widespread and non-essential institutional use of the word *church* creates a perceptual bias and thus favoritism toward members and visitors from Christian backgrounds. This is compounded by otherwise innocent references to *church year*, *church carpet*, *church parking lot*, *church school*, *church office*, *church shopping*, and so on. And this, correspondingly, mutes the UU message and its welcome for those from the "outside."

With deep respect for the histories of Unitarianism and Universalism, and recognizing the comfort and grounding offered by tradition—not to mention the simplicity of a one-syllable word—I accept that the word *church* has its advantages. But the term perpetuates the bias, raises the barrier of entrance, and undermines the sense of welcome for people whose background or perspective is agnostic or atheist, Buddhist, Earth-centered, Hindu, Muslim, Jewish, Native American, or Pagan. These principles also apply to nominal or practicing Christians who feel alienated or otherwise disaffected—this could include those from denominations in which the term *the Church* holds a specific meaning. And while the above list is by no means exhaustive, it could also encompass families in which one partner identifies with one of the labels while the other partner does not.

Historical habit and a non-malicious "majoritarianism" are the likely reasons for the widespread use of the word *church*. But if that's the case, then how does this reconcile with UU efforts to address marginalization? Regarding race, it has been increasingly recognized that people with white skin often do not recognize the privileges associated with their skin color without someone calling attention to it. And it is not uncommon for those in the majority to exhibit a reluctance to acknowledge the privilege when it is pointed out. The UUA "Standing on the Side of Love" and "Welcoming Congregations" programs proclaim that connections and families come in various forms, and that all sexual orientations are to be embraced by our communities. Why isn't there a similar perspective regarding theological and cultural orientations? Why don't I receive the same support if I say, "I don't feel fully welcome here, and I have no good answer when someone asks me, 'What's up with the word *church*?'"

It is not uncommon for UUs of non-Christian backgrounds to be asked whether Unitarian Universalism is a Christian religion. I ask the following related question and wonder why my suggested answer isn't more readily offered:

Question: "If we are a church, why don't we have a cross like almost all other churches?" (Note that more than

99 percent of the "church" listings in the Yellow Pages are Christian; this represents an even higher percentage than the number of dictionary definitions for church that reference Christianity.)

Answer: "We are actually very different from Christian churches, which consider Jesus to be divine and offer ways to access his blessing and your salvation. Do not be misled when you consider joining us for worship or the spiritual work we are engaged in; we are *not* Christian in ritual, dogma, or creed. We are in deep harmony with what have historically been recognized as Christian *principles*: acts of human lovingkindness, embrace of the other, care for the weak, etc. Further, we openly embrace many streams of thought and practice that resonate with such values. This is why those who come to us from Christian, non-Christian, non-Judeo-Christian, or even non-theistic backgrounds feel fully welcomed for inquiry, inspiration, and action."

To me, it is quite obvious that an institution that references *church carpeting* or *church school* doesn't present itself as a community with a high priority for addressing questions that many from non-Christian backgrounds would reasonably ask. This frustrates Unitarian Universalism's desire to be more widely known, understood, and embraced. Sadly, I can't muster enthusiasm for inviting non-Christians to this faith when I don't feel a part of the word *our* when I hear the phrase "our church."

Several years ago I attended a Brotherhood Breakfast at Temple Beth El in Great Neck, New York, where esteemed Rabbi Jerome Davidson made reference to a close relationship between Rabbi Stephen Wise and Unitarian minister John Haynes Holmes. The latter was referred to as a liberal Protestant theologian, and I whispered to my host, "Unitarian." Davidson said that Holmes regarded Jesus as a Jewish historical figure rather than a deity, and that this perspective was compatible with the views of Wise and other liberal Jews of the time. Wise joked that, were there to be any formalization of the relationship between these two men's obviously compatible traditions, Reform Judaism would bear additional criticism from Conservative and Orthodox Jews, who would say, "See, they even go to a church!"

By contrast, someone once quoted former UUA moderator Gini Courter on the Unitarian Universalists for Jewish Awareness email list as saying that we should be working to create a religion so compelling that nobody cares whether our houses of worship are called churches or not. While I initially found her comment combative and offensive, the more I think about it, the more I agree. The problem is that we do not yet have such a religion, and I wonder whether we are on such a path.

Consider the following: I'm in relationship with a lovely woman whose background includes Catholic school and evangelical Christianity. We pray, meditate, share our spirituality, and celebrate our differences together. Thus, we see ourselves as naturally practicing the same religion. Without prompting, she has questioned why should she have any more "leg up," "welcome," or "claim" in coming to Unitarian Universalism than I do.

I find no comfortable answer when family and friends question why a Jew would go to a church. I am puzzled when fellow congregants wonder why a UU would continue to observe significant Jewish holidays. And I am saddened when they express surprise but not curiosity when I say that my ancestors share—although quite separately—a heritage of Romanian religious persecution with members of the Unitarian partner church in Transylvania. In my "elevator speech" about Unitarian Universalism, I describe it as the proper place for me to expand upon my mid-twentieth-century Reform Jewish background in a way that honors my mother and father and offers the gift of my upbringing to a community that speaks of a radical welcome but sometimes falls painfully short of this ambition.

—◦—

RICK FIERBERG *was raised in a community with colonial roots and a strong Jewish presence. He began regularly attending and soon joined The Unitarian Church in Westport, Connecticut, in 2001, where he involved himself in every element of congregational life. He served as a trustee of the Metro New York District for six years as it focused on multiculturalism and moved toward regional governance.*

My New Minyan

Bonnie Zimmer

Sh'Ma Yisrael Adonai Elohainu, Adonai Echad!
"Hear O Israel, the Lord our God, the Lord is One!"

My relationship to the *Shema*, perhaps the most recognizable and well-known prayer in Jewish liturgy is, like much of my relationship to Judaism—complex and contradictory.

The sound of the chant, the lilt of the Hebrew, and the voices joined in unison connect to a part of me so deep I find it difficult to name. When I sing the Shema I see my grandfather's face smiling at me. I can feel my Poppa Max, now forty years dead, slip his hand into mine as we walk together, down East 29th Street, turning left on Avenue N, then right on Nostrand Avenue, walking to temple, every Friday night and every Saturday morning of my childhood. My heart can feel the pride he beamed at me as I sang from the pulpit, reminding me I was his special joy, his *naches*, the one who would continue the traditions he had so tenderly carried with him from his beloved home in Eastern Europe.

As I sing, I feel the power of connection with my temple community as we all rise and chant in unison, some *davenning*, some with eyes closed, all singing at the top of our lungs.

Hear O Israel! I feel a visceral connection to global Judaism, knowing that at that same designated time around the world, Jews would be rising and singing the Shema. As I chant, I also remember the stories I heard growing up in Brooklyn. Stories told by my friends' parents—people who always wore long sleeves to hide the tattooed numbers on their arms. They told stories of those who had not survived. The martyrs, they said, "entered the gas chambers with the Shema on their lips." Less a prayer than a statement of solidarity. A pledge of allegiance to a people some intended to eliminate.

And I also have other feelings about the Shema. While the word Israel (Yisrael) once made me proud of the survival and transcendence of my people, I later understood that the word is also used in ways I feel anything but proud of. A claim of special status. A way to keep others out. A call to war. A claim that *we* are chosen and others are outsiders. So, the call to awaken Israel didn't go far enough for me. I wanted everyone to be awoken. Not just Jews but all of us.

As a humanist Jew, I also felt awkward praying about God—as awkward as I did in school, pledging another kind of allegiance "under God." I have never found spiritual solace or strength in looking outside humanity for repair, healing, and salvation.

And yet, that music! That history! My grandfather's love! That sense of global connection! Those stories of survival and transcendence! They all kept me there, honoring the ancient traditions and my identification with my own small but very proud tribe of humanity.

In Judaism, the connection to other Jews is so important that most rituals require that there be ten Jews gathered before a ritual can begin. This requirement for a *minyan* is one of the many things that can make a Jewish person's journey to Unitarian Universalism so bumpy and complicated. My journey was one of the bumpy ones.

My *bat mitzvah* took place the year Robert Kennedy and Martin Luther King Jr. were assassinated. New York City was burning with racial violence and mistrust. In my public school, I was inspired by tapes of King's speeches and by teachers who were active in the civil rights movement. We were taught that celebrating difference and valuing diversity would show us the way to a new multiracial America.

But in Hebrew school, the lessons were quite different: Stick together. Don't Mix. Never trust the *goyim*. Deep inside, every goy is an anti-Semite waiting to emerge. Will they take our side and protect us when they come to round us up again?

These dire warnings made no sense to me, living as I did in a cross-racial and cross-cultural friendship circle. The lessons of Hebrew school seemed narrow, nationalistic, and ultimately unpalatable. I grew angry and disillusioned. As Conservative Jews, we seemed so committed to honoring history and tradition that we missed the promise and the challenges of what was happening in the modern world around us. Within a year of my bat mitzvah, I left the temple altogether.

Life went on and eventually I met Jim, now my spouse of more than twenty years, a self-defined recovering Catholic from Wisconsin who had an affinity for scholars from the Jewish left, and, luckily for me, for Jewish women as well! We loved creating our own rituals. Each year, we hosted a magical Passover *Seder* at my family's beachfront cottage in southern Maine. The minyan gathered there included gay and straight folks, Jews and non-Jews, young people, older relatives, and babies as they arrived on the scene. I felt content.

And then the birth of my son Alex transformed me into a Jewish mother. I felt a powerful need to nurture in him a strong, positive Jewish identity. Jim was happy to raise our child Jewish, as he had no similar passion for passing on his religious heritage. But we wondered how we could help Alex feel good about all of who he was. How could we find a spiritual education that wouldn't contradict the lessons he was learning in his multiracial, public elementary school?

We tried a number of alternative Jewish groups who catered to interfaith families. Yet, under the surface we continued to feel an intangible sense of us versus them. When Alex was only four years old, he said, "Mom, I don't feel like these people really accept my daddy." So we began searching yet again for a minyan that welcomed all of us, not just willingly but joyfully.

Jim started visiting Unitarian Universalist congregations. I occasionally accompanied him, but the Jew in me recoiled at the Christian feel of the places we visited: the buildings, the music, the quiet, how polite everyone seemed. Where were the minor chords? Where was the modal scale that moved my soul? Where were the loud discussions and arguments that accompany Jewish gatherings? Why did it feel so much like church? If Unitarian Universalists honor our Judeo-Christian heritage, why was it so hard for me to see and feel the Judeo part?

Still, in the spring of 2001, I stumbled into First Parish in Arlington, Massachusetts, on a Sunday morning. The minister was conducting a live survey of the congregation. "Stand if you agree with the statements I am about to read," she said. "And don't censor the urge to stand in support of a statement which completely contradicts the one you stood for a moment ago. Just listen and stand (or do this motion) if you agree with each statement." After many intriguing questions, she then said, "Stand if you agree with the following: I would like it if there were more Jewish ritual here." My memory is that at least half of the congregation either stood or waved their hands.

"Wow! They must all be Jews," I thought. I scanned their profiles for the telltale nose, the kinky Semitic hair. I searched the order of service for names like Stein and Goldberg. But I found that, while some were Jews, most were not. The congregation was laughing self-lovingly at their many internal contradictions. And the minister was smiling, enjoying every minute of it. She clearly loved this messy, conflicted, contradictory gathering of humanity. And alongside other wishes for the future, they longed for more Jewish ritual, just like me! I was intrigued. Yet in the end, I just couldn't bring myself back to a place called *church*.

Then, four months later, on a sunny Tuesday morning, the twin towers in my hometown were knocked out of the sky. My eighty-year-old mother watched from her bus window on the way to work as the second plane exploded, and it would be several agonizing hours before I got word that she was alive and safe. I sensed that, this time, music and ritual alone would not be enough to get me through. I needed people around me who, like me, were struggling to find meaning. The world was changing in ways beyond anything I could imagine.

I came to realize that I yearned for a spiritual community. So that Sunday, September 16, 2001, I had my second religious experience at First Parish. Sitting among strangers with Jim, I listened to the minister, Kathy Huff, give voice to my anger, my outrage, my stark terror, my confusion, and my grief. I sobbed among a minyan of strangers and felt perfectly safe. Someone sitting next to me put her arm around me and held me as I cried. When Kathy ended her sermon with a quote from the diary of Anne Frank, I knew I had found a place where my husband and daughter and I could find connection and meaning in this newly broken world.

The journey is still sometimes painful for the Jewish part of me. Language remains a problem. Coming to a place called *church* is both historically and personally challenging. So I take liberties with translation. Rather than my *church*, it is my *congregation*. I miss Jewish music. I long to hear the kvetching and whining of a good cantor. Sometimes I want Alex to have a *bar mitzvah*, not a coming of age ceremony. I love Jewish weddings and find profound comfort in Jewish burial and mourning rituals. And sometimes, out of nowhere, although I love my congregation and feel more and more a part of its fabric, a sudden sense of alienation and loneliness will sneak up and surprise me.

The Jewish Connections Group, which I helped to organize my first year at First Parish, meets what some of us call our genetic need to affiliate with other Jews. Yet I realize that I actually feel most myself right in the midst of the congregation, where I can feel all of who I am: a Jew and all the other parts, in all my still-defining, contradictory, wrestling humanity. It is all my fellow congregants, in the end, who have become my new minyan.

As it turns out, the Hebrew word *Yisrael* means "one who wrestles." How Unitarian Universalist! How Jewish! With thanks to Kahal B'raira, the Boston congregation for Humanistic Judaism, I offer us this alternative translation as we sing together: Hear all you who wrestle! Our people are One. Humanity is One.

Sh'Ma Yisrael Adonai Elohainu, Adonai Echad! Amen.

-◄o►-

BONNIE ZIMMER *attends First Parish Unitarian Universalist in Arlington, Massachusetts. For more than twenty years she has used her clinical social work training in her work to support and advocate for survivors of domestic violence. Together with her partner of twenty-five years, Bonnie is the proud parent of an eighteen-year-old son who was raised as a Jewish Unitarian Universalist.*

AUTHENTICALLY CYNICAL

PAUL DAVID WADLER

I have many experiences of joy as a Jewish Unitarian Universalist. These include participating in rituals from my childhood such as celebrating *Seder*, lighting the *menorah* or shaking the *lulav* in diverse racial groups, young and old. I did not feel I had to hide my cynicism at the biblical injunctions or listen to the hilariously ridiculous and frustrating *halakhic* discussions of my family—straight out of a Woody Allen movie—of how or when or where or by whom the ritual was to be performed. I could breathe in the mystical spirituality—without all the *meshugass*—in a community of like-minded spiritual seekers. Such a joy!

I was raised in a *kosher* home in rural South Texas by parents who thought it was vital for me to have a strong sense of my Jewish identity. This was the Bible Belt, where prayers to Jesus were regularly recited at school and opened every football game. It was not easy to keep a traditional Jewish household when the nearest kosher meat was sixty miles away, in Houston. But my parents were very intentional about doing so and our small rural town had a synagogue and rabbi and drew from about a hundred Jewish families in southeast coastal Texas.

I came to understand myself as separate from all those around me. It was like living a parallel existence, observing the Christian world from the mezzanine of life's theater, never feeling completely part of it. My family was surrounded by Bible-thumping, well-meaning people who had absolutely no interest in our religious identity or our heritage. It was unthinkable that I could be Jewish and simultaneously a part of a religious community of diverse people.

As I entered college, the religious tenets of Judaism began to mean less and less to me. I certainly didn't believe Jews were a chosen people or that some external being was keeping score of whether or not I ate pork or how many times I *davened*. And I began to learn about the Christian religion that had surrounded me my whole life, but that I had never gotten to know. I had learned to be as suspicious of Christians in Texas as my ancestors must have been, living hundreds of years ago in the *shtetls* of Eastern Europe. I had been subjected to the harsh side of Christianity. I knew they blamed my people for killing their G-d. But over time I learned about the centrality of love and forgiveness in much of the Christian tradition. And I came to understand the central messages in other religious traditions.

As I grew further away from the faith in which I had been brought up, I felt I could not fully participate in religious community. I could not be fully Jewish and recite prayers to a G-d I didn't believe existed, and I couldn't fully participate in any other faith community because I was Jewish, despite my lack of belief. I struggled with what I perceived as elitism in the exclusionary nature of Jewish community. Non-Jews were Other and I should never completely trust them. Coming out as a gay man threw yet another wrinkle in the equation.

And then I discovered Unitarian Universalism—a faith community where I could be fully Jewish, but where I could be authentically cynical about the supernatural parts of the religion—G-d speaking through burning bushes and ordering Abraham to kill his son, for example—that I couldn't bring myself to believe. It was a community of seekers that accepted me for who I am, no questions asked. Nothing in my experience of being Unitarian Universalist has been greater than the personal joy of finding that such a community existed.

I can throw my whole self into Christian, Hindu, Native American, and other religious rituals fully, without feeling like I am sacrificing or hiding my Jewish heritage. Whether in my own congregation or at General Assembly, worshipping with UUs from around the country, I feel I can respectfully celebrate diverse religious traditions with little fear of misappropriating or, worse, feeling cynically hypocritical. Unitarian Universalism gives me a unique vantage point from which I can maintain my own Jewish tradition and belief—or lack of belief—with integrity, while having a transcendent experience participating in another tradition's ritual.

I have had those transcendent experiences in religious rituals, but what has surprised me the most is that when I shed the baggage of my religious past, Jewish rituals take on new meanings within a Unitarian Universalist context. The annual Seders at my congregation, where we link the Exodus to civil rights and human rights and LGBT rights are so much more meaningful to me than the arguments over what kinds of grains we are permitted to eat during Passover. In some ways, being a Unitarian Universalist has made me be a better and more appreciative Jew.

I have studied the *Torah* and *Talmud* as a Unitarian Universalist and seen the most sacred texts of my people through new eyes. Freed from considering whether or not the texts are G-d's special message to G-d's special people, I can read these texts for their spiritual message, written by a people and transmitted from generation to generation over thousands of years to their descendants. Given my belief that there is no personal G-d and no giving of the Torah on Mount Sinai, I can ask, Why were these texts written? By whom and for whom? What did it mean that these people called themselves chosen? Why did they invent the G-d they did?

So I have felt profound joy in Unitarian Universalism and Unitarian Universalism has helped me find joy and meaning in Judaism. However, I have felt alienation and even pain as well. Unitarian Universalism takes very seriously the suffering of the disempowered. For example, we agonize over how we contribute to the oppression of people of color and frequently examine the issue of white privilege both within our personal lives and within our movement. We accept that our movement, with its lily-white pedigree of Unitarianism and Universalism, has much to undo regarding white privilege in order to be the inclusive movement we aim to be.

Unitarian Universalism emerged from the educated, white, middle-class Christian Unitarians and the more down-to-earth, white, middle-class and working-class Christian Universalists. We examine how coming out of the middle-class white community has left us with baggage we must contend with, but we rarely examine what it means to come out of Christianity and who might be left out. I have not seen nearly as rigorous an examination of Christian privilege within our movement and how the assumption of Christianity has kept religious and ethnic diversity out of our congregations. In fact, I have seen tremendous resistance to such examination.

Christian supremacy is as much a threat to diversity and liberation as white supremacy. We fail to address the thread of Christian assumptions running through our movement at our peril. Do Unitarian Universalists need to take a stand against Palestinian oppression? Of course we do. But when we do, we need to be sensitive to the fact that the oppressive Israelis are responding to oppression of their own—an oppression in which we are complicit. Anti-Semitism and

Christian supremacy are one and the same. It seems that at virtually every UU General Assembly, delegates are asked to condemn Palestinian oppression. Yet when condemning the Israeli government, we become complicit in creating an environment in which anti-Semitism may flourish.

Anti-Semitism exists where Christian supremacy is assumed. UUs may recognize the anti-Semitism inherent in the annual right wing blathering of the supposed "War on Christmas." Most of us recognize the immorality of insisting that everyone is wished "Merry Christmas" rather than the more inclusive "Happy Holidays." To make other religions and traditions invisible, to assume Christianity as the default religion, works against the inclusive beloved community for which Unitarian Universalists strive.

Just as Unitarian Universalists have scoured our hymnals for sexist, racist, and homophobic language, we need to faithfully and thoroughly examine the many ways in which we marginalize Jews and Judaism and privilege Christianity within our movement. Naming our congregations *churches*, holding services on Sundays, using Protestant liturgies and Protestant hymns are just some of the ways in which we ensure that white Protestants have a seamless experience entering our congregations, and that others feel alienated.

I know that Unitarian Universalists want to be better. I know that our ideals far outstrip our abilities. I can imagine Unitarian Universalism contending with the issues that make me feel excluded as a Jew and adopting religious inclusivism as a fundamental goal of our movement. The news of the world shows us that religious inclusion and respect for all religions is a central issue for the world today. For example, Muslim-bashing has become commonplace. Unitarian Universalists can help lead a movement that changes the world for the better.

Just as we lead in the fights for racial equality, gender equality, and LGBT equality, we are poised to lead in the struggle for religious inclusiveness and mutual respect between and among religions. Just as I struggle with imperfections and limitations, so do we all. I believe deep in my heart that my fellow Unitarian Universalists want me in this movement and in their congregations, just as I want them. I believe that the insults I experience are no more personal than the slights I may inflict upon my fellow congregants. Unitarian Universalism is by definition idealistic. I comfort myself by holding onto the idea that we can always become more perfect.

◄o►

PAUL DAVID WADLER *is a clinical psychologist in Chicago, specializing in helping LGBT individuals and same-sex couples. He holds a master of divinity degree from Harvard Divinity School. He has served as board chair for Second Unitarian in Chicago, and served on the board and as district vice president of the Central Midwest District. Most recently, he served as vice chair of the UUA Ministerial Fellowship Committee from 2004 to 2011.*

LEAVEN AND HORSERADISH

MARTI KELLER

One Saturday evening in the winter of 2011, several dozen people gathered for a *Havdalah* service for the ending of the Jewish Sabbath. They stood for evening prayer, they witnessed the smelling of sweet and pungent spices to fortify the soul for the new week, they chanted and swayed in ecstatic *Hasidic* fashion. They were Jewish Unitarian Universalists from all over the country. They worshipped in a modernistic Unitarian Universalist sanctuary, designed in bowl style, with a skylight and stark walls. This was not the worship of our Boston Brahmin fathers, not anything Channing or Emerson would have ever seen in their wood-pew New England churches. Certainly not anything my Jewish humanist parents would have seen in their Unitarian fellowship in suburban Maryland, with its speaker's lectern and string quartets.

Truth be told, this traditional, if beautifully adapted, Jewish service is not what they would have wanted. Even before they married, each had come to the conclusion that religious Judaism had nothing to offer them and cultural Jewishness almost nothing—except, in my father's case, a more than occasional craving for cold red beet *borscht* with a generous dollop of sour cream, for some pickled herring, and for the Jewish comedians Jack Benny, Mort Sahl, and Lenny Bruce.

My father also loved the baseball player Hank Greenberg, who proved that Jewish boys could hit and catch and, despite the prejudice they encountered, become major league stars. I was reminded of this recently at the opening night of the Atlanta Jewish Festival at the Fox Theater in downtown Atlanta, where more than three thousand people bought tickets to see *Jews in Baseball*. Before the movie began, we stood for the national anthem, hands over hearts, and sang "Take Me Out to the Ballgame," first in English, then in Yiddish, led by a local rabbi, learning that this emblematic American song, like so many others, was written by a Jew.

But in that moment of rising and singing and uniting around the national pastime, we were primarily living out the Protestant, Catholic, Jewish, American paradigm—an assimilated, universalized identity that marked my childhood and so many others'. This alphabet-soup melting pot was held together by sports and patriotism—a recipe for a society that recognized that there were non-Protestants in the soup as benign flavorings, but that still preferenced a kind of cultural Christianity.

This was the world my family created for their post-World War II children, with its brick ranch houses and Scout troops and Fourth of July fireworks and cook-outs. The world of our cul-de-sac neighborhood, in which every house had a Christmas tree and every child found Easter baskets on our beds and hunted for eggs. A world where every morning in school we said the Pledge of Allegiance for one nation under a God who didn't mind Jews, but where the songs we sang for holiday choir concerts were always Christian.

I grew up in a culturally Christian world, including my religious home, chosen for me by my parents—a fledgling Unitarian church. The congregation renamed it a *church* after it left its small temporary digs in a women's club, bought its own stand of woods, and built its modern building with its large glass windows looking out at what is sometimes called the Cathedral of the World. The minister did not wear a clerical robe, at least most of the time, and there were no formal pews and no organ—at least at first. But downstairs, in the religious education program, the teachers prepared us to visit "The Church Across the Street." Not the synagogue, and certainly not the mosque.

I didn't just visit those churches. I sang in their choirs with my girlfriends, lustily singing traditional hymns and gospel music while hardly hearing a word of Hebrew. This was *my* Jewish Unitarian upbringing. Not until I had children and started my own family did I begin a very tentative exploration of my Jewishness. My initial experiences with synagogue worship were as unfamiliar as a Catholic Latin Mass, perhaps even more.

In 2011, my congregation in Atlanta hosted the second-ever national meeting of Unitarian Universalists for Jewish Awareness. The first one took place more than twenty years earlier. We came together, as the name of the gathering promised, "to be counted," to know that those of us who identify as Jewish are not isolated and unseen. We came to affirm that we matter to each other and to our larger liberal religious movement, with its commitment to diversity, to multiculturalism, and to being a multi-source faith tradition. We gathered to hear each other's stories and to ask each other how we found our way into Unitarian Universalist congregations, why we have stayed, what gives us joy and a sense of belonging, and also what challenges us, troubles us, and might indeed make us leave. We assembled to question what it means to be both Jewish and Unitarian Universalist.

In preparation for our time together, I revisited the subject of an honors thesis I completed a dozen years earlier as part of my master of divinity studies at Candler School of Theology at Emory University. Titled *Inside or Outside the Fold: The Circumstances Under Which Jews Join the Unitarian Universalist Congregation of Atlanta*, the thesis was a participant observer study. I selected the Atlanta congregation as the research site, the faith community where I had been a member prior to studying for the ministry, where our youngest son had been in the religious education program, where I had served in the first class of lay ministers, and where I had become involved with the I'Chaim Jewish Celebrations and Awareness Group, helping to craft some of their worship materials. While I observed the activities conducted by the Jewish members there and interviewed them about their spiritual and cultural journeys, I did not set aside my own affiliation with the congregation or my own quest. These congregants and I wrestled with the same issues.

My studies and observations over the years demonstrate that, if there is any one thing that initially keeps Jewish people out of our faith movement and continues to trouble us once we join, it is the use of the word *church*—even in congregations, fellowships, and meeting houses that do not call themselves a church. Other commonly used Christian words can be also be discomforting, or at least require a fair amount of translation, such as *ministry*, *parish*, and *grace*. Trigger words like these—*church*, in particular—can require a major transition. They can stir up a wrenching confrontation with a worldview, ritual system, and symbolic universe that can be greatly disturbing to Jews, who have a history of persecution and terror in the Jewish-Christian struggle.

Language matters. And it can keep people on the other side of the wall and outside our doors. But some of us have crossed the threshold. So my questions for myself and those I have studied and met over the years include whether we who identify as Jewish UUs come from similar religious backgrounds and cultural practices. What attracted us to this congregation or others, and in order to join a UU society, what types of accommodations did we need to make? What did we know about the Jews within Unitarian Universalism? How are we counted by our own religious association and by the Jewish community at large?

It turns out that we know very little about our numbers. The percentage of Jewish Unitarian Universalists within the American Jewish population is not specifically tracked in the Jewish Population Study. Instead, we are lumped into the categories "born/raised Jewish," or "switched to another religion," or "adults of Jewish background," or "other current religion." The core Jewish population, targeted by most Jewish community agencies, includes only three identities: those who are born Jews and report their current religion as Jewish, those who are Jews by choice, or those who are born Jews and report having no current religion. These identities represent about 90 percent of the American Jewish population. On the ground, that means we are invisible to Jewish federations and other Jewish-connected political and charitable institutions who might want to reach out to us, to learn about our sense of identity and theology. So we show up at film festivals, Jewish Museums, and other cultural/religious assemblages of Jewish people under our own steam, by our own initiative.

Unitarian Universalist Association archival information on Jewish UUs is also sparse. When I wrote my thesis, the most recent denominational survey that collected data on religion of origin was more than twenty years old, listing Jews as 4 percent of the total UU membership. This survey might have missed Jews whose families of origin considered themselves ethnically or culturally Jewish but not religiously Jewish. The Jewish UUs surveyed in the past have not been asked, at least for a study, how they sub-identify—from which Jewish denomination they have come, if any.

In addition to this lack of statistical data, the UUA has never conducted any in depth study of Jews within the Association. When the Commission on Appraisal listed marginalized groups as an issue of concern for the growth and vitality of congregations, Jews were not considered as among them, even though the Commission's definition of a marginal group included lower proportional representation and a sense that the group must fight for recognition of their perspectives and interests. We often feel—and this is supported by evidence—that indeed we are not counted, or not in ways that recognize who we are, with the identities we carry.

The UU Jews who took part in my thesis research came from Reform, Orthodox, Conservative, what one person described as Southern Conservative, born and raised UU Jewish, and humanist/atheist Jewish backgrounds. Many are married to Christians. Asked to describe their current religious identity, they reported themselves as secular humanist, Jewish UU, Jewish who attend a UU congregation, raised Jewish who attend a UU congregation, "Jewnitarian," or simply Unitarian Universalist. Some were born and raised in atheist families like mine, where their parents had already decided to disconnect from Jewish tradition, at least religiously. For those who were previously connected to a Jewish congregation, some of the reasons for leaving included disenchantment with the messages and practices, disillusionment with rabbinical authority, and in some instances, the refusal of rabbis and congregations to recognize intermarriage.

Why did we want to be counted as Unitarian Universalists? Only three of the twenty-two Jewish people interviewed for the study reported that they sought a belief system and a faith community that made sense. For most, the UU acceptance of intermarriage or the need for a religious home for their children where they could receive a balanced, multi-source education were far more important. Respondents had done little or no reading or other information-gathering about Unitarian Universalism, about the beliefs and principles of the faith, or about the congregation. Their exposure primarily consisted of word of mouth from friends or neighbors.

Other reasons for joining our congregations included a perception of inclusiveness—that Unitarian Universalists do not adhere to a creed. Some reported wanting to be part of a larger community of liberal congregants who yearn for spiritual peace and community and a sense of belonging. Others were attracted by our social justice history and work, consistent with the Jewish principle of *tikkun olam*, or repairing the world. Other values that seemed specifically

Jewish included the responsibility to take care of neighbors and the poor, the significance of education, and the support of families of all kinds.

Respondents also told of the challenges they faced in Unitarian Universalist congregations. Some described the difficulty of holding onto certain Jewish traditions without the guilt. Some said the challenge was making peace with our families and with the decision, in the eyes of others, to leave the conventional Jewish fold. We struggle sometimes with two poles on the spectrum of experience: on one hand, feeling like outsiders having to pass or hide our religious and cultural identities; on the other hand, becoming the identified Jews within a congregation, called upon to "represent" religious orientations, history, culture, and political viewpoints as if Jews have a monolithic perspective. Collectively, UU Jews feel the need for more Jewish content, claiming, celebrating, and sharing not just the major holidays but the deeper spiritual gifts of Judaism—what we often call moving "beyond the *menorah*" and a kind of ritual tokenism.

My study of Jews in our faith tradition led me to want to do further research on how we, as individuals and as a Jewish presence within Unitarian Universalism, could more actively participate in fostering an authentic multiculturalism. The answers might include confronting the stereotypes and prejudices espoused by UUs—thus truly living into acceptance and diversity. Much of the consideration of Jews within Unitarian Universalism—and also of other groups who leave one fold to join this one—focuses on what they have to leave behind and how they accommodate to our culture, with only a minor acknowledgment of their particular gifts to us. Rather than accept and expect neutral assimilation or get approached as yet another challenging subgroup, we are compelled to more fully share what Rabbi Arthur Green calls "our creative, dissonant Jewish culture, our contrarian history as questioners and challengers of society's grand assumptions and value systems, as idol smashers." We are called to help teach and live out the values of justice and decency embodied, as he tells us, in our prophetic heritage. In return, we hope to more fully be recognized as an essential leaven in this living faith tradition (except at Passover, when we can be the horseradish).

◄○►

MARTI KELLER *has served as a minister in both community and parish settings for fifteen years, most recently at the Unitarian Universalist Congregation of Atlanta, Georgia. She is also a past president of Unitarian Universalists for Jewish Awareness, an at-large member of the board of the Society for Humanistic Judaism, and a contributor to their journal.*

GLOSSARY

The following terms are from Hebrew, unless otherwise indicated.

There are no official rules or uniform standards for transliterating Hebrew letters and words into the English alphabet. Due to the variety of transliteration schemes, there are often different transcriptions for the same Hebrew word, depending on the culture or ethnicity of the user: Ashkenazi, Sephardic, Mitzrahi, Israeli, etc. For purposes of uniformity, the editors have selected one transliteration of Hebrew words.

Adonai. Literally, "my Lord." Since early times this term has been used to replace Y-H-W-H, described in the Torah as the hidden, mysterious name of God which is forbidden to be spoken.

Akedah. The name given to the story in Genesis about Abraham's attempt to sacrifice his son Isaac on Mt. Moriah.

Aleynu. Prayer of divine sovereignty, originally part of the Rosh Hashanah service, added as the conclusion to all services. See *Rosh Hashanah*.

Ashkenazi. Jewish people of Eastern European descent.

Bar Mitzvah. The male coming of age ritual performed for boys aged thirteen years and older. Literally "subject to the law," the ritual transfers the responsibility for Jewish law, rituals, and traditions from parents to son.

Bat Mitzvah. The female coming of age ritual performed for girls aged thirteen years and older. Literally "subject to the law," the ritual transfers the responsibility for Jewish law, rituals, and traditions from parents to daughter.

Bimah. The raised platform from which services are conducted.

Btzelem elohim. In the divine image.

Chabad. One of the largest and best known Hasidic movements of Orthodox Judaism. See *Hasidism*.

Chad Gadya. Literally "one little goat" or "one kid." A playful song often sung during the Seder or ritual meal at the beginning of Passover. See *Pesach*.

Challah. The sweet Jewish bread traditionally eaten on the Sabbath. See *Sabbath*.

Chanukah. A historical Jewish holiday commemorating the defeat of the Greek Syrians by the Maccabees. Also spelled *Hanukkah*.

Charoset. A mixture of apples or other fruits, nuts, wine and spices put on the Seder plate to symbolize the mortar Jewish slaves used when they were building for the Egyptians. See *Seder*.

Daven. Yiddish word meaning to pray, especially to chant liturgical prayers.

Drash. Sermon on Friday nights.

Dreidel. A wooden toy played with during Chanukah. See *Chanukah*.

Erev. Evening. Jewish days (and holidays) begin in the evening, at sunset.

Erev rav. Literally "a mixed multitude." The phrase used in Exodus to describe the community that left Egypt at the end of the plagues.

Haggadah. Literally "narrative." The text used for the Seder, a ritual meal typically conducted at home during the first two evenings of Passover. See *Pesach*.

Halakhah. Literally "the path" or "the walking." The system of Jewish religious praxis as codified in laws developed by generations of scholars about how to understand the Torah. See *Torah*.

Hamentaschen. Triangle-shaped pastries traditionally eaten during the Jewish holiday of Purim. See *Purim*.

Hasid. An individual who practices Hasidism.

Hasidism. A branch of Orthodox Judaism that promotes spirituality through the internalization of Jewish mysticism. Derived from *hesed*, which literally means "a free flowing love that knows no bounds." Established by Rabbi Israel Bal Shem Tov in Eastern Europe in the eighteenth century.

Havdalah. Literally "separation." A ceremony marking the end of the Jewish Sabbath and the beginning of the new week. The ritual involves lighting a special candle with several wicks, blessing a cup of wine, and smelling sweet spices. See *Sabbath*.

Hora. A traditional round dance of Romania and Israel.

Kabbalah. A type of Jewish mysticism rooted in the teachings of Rabbi Isaac Luria.

Kaddish. An ancient Aramaic prayer in praise of God's powers, recited as prayers for the dead and at other points in a prayer service.

Kavannah. Inner direction or concentration, particularly in prayer. Meditation or prayer before a holy act.

Keva. The set texts of Jewish liturgy.

Kippah. A skullcap worn by Orthodox male Jews at all times, and others for prayer services and religious studies. Also called a Yarmulke.

Kugel. A sweet baked casserole made with noodles or potatoes, eggs, and cottage cheese.

Kvetching. Yiddish word meaning to squeeze, press, urge, complain.

Latkes. Yiddish word for potato pancakes traditionally eaten during the Chanukah festival. The oil for cooking the latkes is symbolic of the oil from the Chanukah story. See *Chanukah*.

L'chah Dodi. Literally, "Come, my beloved." The Friday evening song welcoming the Sabbath as if a queen, or a bride. There are many melodies to the text.

Lulav. A date palm branch, one of the four species carried for the festival of Sukkot. See *Sukkot*.

Maggid. The common meaning is itinerant or popular preacher or storyteller. On Passover, the Maggid is the spontaneous response to the traditional four questions asked as part of the Seder Haggadah. See *Seder* and *Haggadah*.

Mazel Tov. Congratulations. Also a Yiddish word.

Matzah. Unleavened bread eaten during Passover. See *Pesach*.

Menorah. A lamp or candelabrum, either seven or eight lights, derived from the shape of a burning or lighted tree. The eight-light menorah is used during Chanukah to commemorate the eight days and nights the Temple lamp remained lit with only one day's worth of oil. See *Chanukah*.

Meshugass. Yiddish word for craziness.

Mezuzah. A small container or casing holding a scroll of parchments with paragraphs of the Shema attached to the doorstops of a house. See *Shema*.

Mechitza. The partition between men and women in Orthodox and some Conservative Judaism sanctuaries.

Midrash. A form of rabbinic literature that interprets the Torah. See *Torah*.

Minyan. A quorum for prayer. Traditionally ten Jewish males, or today in many Jewish circles ten persons. Only in the presence of a minyan can some prayers, such as the Mourner's Kaddish, be recited.

Mishnah. The first standardized compilation of rabbinic teachings.

Niggun. A mystical, wordless musical prayer introduced by the Hasidim. See *Hasidism*.

Pesach. Passover. A seven-day celebration of spring, liberation, and renewal commemorating the Exodus from Egypt. The first two nights, during the Seder, there is the retelling of the legacy of slavery and the memory of liberation. During this time, no food with leaven may be eaten. For traditional Jews, all leavened food, including crumbs, must be removed from the house. See *Seder*.

Purim. Holiday celebrating the deliverance of the Jewish people from the wicked Haman in the days of Queen Esther of Persia.

Rosh Hashanah. Literally, "head of the year." The beginning of a period of judgment and remembrance, rebirth and renewal called the Days of Awe. Known familiarly as the Jewish New Year.

Seder. Ritual Passover meal.

Shehecheyanu. A blessing, offering thanks for new and unusual experiences.

Shabbat. The Jewish Sabbath, beginning Friday at sunset and ending Saturday at sunset.

Shavuot. Also known as the Feast of Weeks, this occurs fifty-one days after the beginning of Passover. Described in the Hebrew Bible as an agricultural festival, it is now an observance of the giving of the Torah at Mt. Sinai. In Reform Judaism, confirmation ceremonies typically coincide with this holiday. See *Passover* and *Torah*.

Shema. A proclamation that stands at the center of Jewish worship, the essential declaration of traditional Jewish faith: "Hear O Israel, the Lord our God, the Lord is one." It is recited during morning and evening prayer, and inscribed on scrolls in the mezuzah, and in the tefillin. See *Tefillin*.

Shiva. The seven-day period of intense mourning following the death of a close relative. Family and members of the community are urged to visit and console the mourners. The wearing of shoes and sitting in comfortable chairs is forbidden.

Shoah. Literally "catastrophe." In Israel the word is used to describe the Holocaust, the killing of six million Jewish people during the regime of Germany's Third Reich.

Shofar. Ram's horn blown on Rosh Hashanah and Yom Kippur. See *Rosh Hashanah* and *Yom Kippur*.

Shukel. To pray by vigorously bending and moving.

Shul. Yiddish word meaning house of worship or synagogue.

Siddur. A prayer book, printed or written, of the fixed prayer service for ordinary weekdays and Sabbaths.

Sukkot. A harvest festival of the first full moon, during which Sukkah, temporary huts, become the symbolic or real dwelling place for seven days.

Tallis. A fringed prayer shawl. Also *Tallit*.

Talmud. Literally "the learning." The Jewish compendium of law, wisdom, folklore, and everyday life from the early centuries of the Common Era.

Tanakh. The Hebrew Bible, composed of three sections: Torah, Prophets, and Writings. See *Torah*.

Tashlich. Literally "casting off." A ritual that many Jews observe during Rosh Hashanah. It involves symbolically casting off the sins of the previous year by tossing pieces of bread or other food into a body of flowing water. Just as the water carries away the bits of food, so too are sins symbolically carried away. In this way, the participant hopes to start the New Year with a clean slate.

Tefillin. Holy boxes containing biblical passages, worn mainly by Orthodox Jews during weekday morning prayers.

Teshuvah. Repentance for trespasses and transgressions, seeking forgiveness or returning to observance.

Tikkun. To repair or restore. *Tikkun olam* means restoring or mending the world for the betterment of all.

Torah. Literally "teaching." The five books of Moses in the Hebrew Bible.

Tu B'Sishvat. The birthday of the trees.

V'ahavta. The Biblical verse following the Shema "Hear O Israel," namely, "You shall love the eternal . . . " (Deuteronomy 6:5). It is sung during the Sabbath service.

Y-H-W-H. The hidden, mysterious name of God revealed to Moses at the burning bush to send him on his mission (Exodus 3:15). Never pronounced.

Yom Kippur. The Day of Atonement, the holiest day on the Hebrew calendar, "a Sabbath of Sabbaths" on which all work is forbidden. It is a full fast day and is associated with other special prohibitions. It is a day to ask for forgiveness, both of others and of God.

Zohar. *The Book of Splendor*, a Kabbalistic book from thirteenth-century Spain.

ACKNOWLEDGMENTS

I am indebted to many hands and hearts and relationships! I extend deep gratitude to:

my co-conspirator and partner in this project, Marti Keller;

our Skinner House editors, Mary Benard and Marshall Hawkins, who thrilled us beyond belief with this opportunity;

eagle-eyed Emily Morine Johnson, for her quick editing assistance;

each person who has been a part of the UUs for Jewish Awareness (UUJA) community on the Internet and phone, in person and spirit (including those who advised and cheered for this book in capacities other than writing an essay);

those with whom I've served on the UUJA Board of Trustees: Kelly Weisman Asprooth-Jackson, Linda Berez, Deb Cohen, Myrtle McMahan, Mark De Solla Price, Arthur Thexton, and Jay Wolin;

faculty, staff, and students at Starr King School for the Ministry;

the supportive staff, including Roger Bertschausen, and gracious members and friends of Fox Valley Unitarian Universalist Fellowship in Appleton, Wisconsin;

and three couples whose respective partnerships across difference have given me more than I can express: my parents, Sylvia and Marty Hart-Landsberg; my parents-in-law, David and Nancy Ongiri; and my friends Lucila Canul and Britta Houser.

—LHL

My gratitude to Rev. Leah Hart-Landsberg for her dedication to and creative partnership in this project of lifting up Jewish voices in our shared faith tradition.

I remember and continue to give thanks to the late Dr. Nancy Eisland for her encouragement and insights she gave me in researching and writing the honors Masters Thesis (Candler School of Theology, Emory University) that was the basis for my further work in the arena of Jewish presence in Unitarian Universalism.

Thanks to the Jewish members of the Unitarian Universalist Congregation of Atlanta for sharing their religious journeys.

—MK